A BULL BY T
BACK DOOR

A Bull by the Back Door

by Anne Loader

Illustrated by Patricia Kelsall

An imprint of
ANNE LOADER
PUBLICATIONS

Dedicated with grateful thanks
to **Joan Ward, Léonie Dutheil**
and **Joyce Crust**
who made this book possible

ISBN
1 901253 06 6

First published October 1997
Reprinted December 1997
Reprinted March 1999
Reprinted September 2000
Reprinted March 2005

Published by:
Léonie Press
an imprint of
Anne Loader Publications
13 Vale Road, Hartford
Northwich, Cheshire CW8 1PL
Gt Britain
Tel: 01606 75660   Fax: 01606 77609
e-mail: anne@leoniepress.com
Website: www.leoniepress.com

Origination by Anne Loader Publications
Covers laminated by The Finishing Touch, St Helens
Printed by Poplar Services, St Helens

About the author and illustrator

Anne Loader is a writer and publisher. She was born in
Lincolnshire in 1948 and trained as a journalist with East
Midland Allied Press in Spalding and King's Lynn from 1965-68.
In 1969 she married Jack Loader who was doing a PhD in
Chemistry at Southampton University. She worked at the
Southern Evening Echo until they moved to Cheshire in 1970
when he took up his job as a research scientist in the chemical
industry. They had two sons and for the next ten years Anne
worked from home as a writer and printer. She edited and
contributed to *Pregnancy and Parenthood* on behalf of The
National Childbirth Trust, which was published by OUP in 1980.
The same year she returned to journalism as a feature writer on
Northwich World and in 1984 she helped to start the *World* local
newspaper in Crewe, becoming editor in 1985. It later became
the *Crewe and Nantwich Guardian*. She was made redundant as
editor in 1995 and in 1996 she set up as a freelance writer and
page designer. Shortly afterwards, she started the Léonie Press
as an imprint of Anne Loader Publications, specialising in
producing books on local history and autobiography.

Patricia Kelsall is a part-time lecturer in Art & Design at Mid-
Cheshire College teaching drawing and painting to full-time and
part-time students. She has exhibited her work mainly in the
North East of England and in Cheshire as well as the Royal
Academy in London, the Manchester Academy of Fine Art and
at the Annual Salon in Mornant, France. Patricia's illustrations
and paintings have appeared in numerous publications including
Newcastle 900 by Frank Graham, greetings card designs for
Bucentaur Gallery and many limited edition publications includ-
ing publicity brochures, letterheads, menus and local authority
town trail leaflets. Her paintings have been reviewed in *The
Observer Magazine* and *The Guardian* newspaper. She loves visiting
France and she and her artist-husband Richard have spent many
Summer holidays in France where they enjoy walking combined
with outdoor sketching and painting.

A Bull by the Back Door

Everything described in this book is true, to the best of my knowledge. However to protect the privacy of our friends in France I have changed their names and the names of the villages mentioned. They were kind to us because they are marvellous people — not because they thought they would be the subjects of a book. We thank them from the bottom of our hearts.

Anne Loader

List of illustrations

Contents

This time the bull meant business – the herd was staying.

iii

Introduction

The Limousin bull was massive, battle-scarred and very well hung.

One of his horns was twisted. He swaggered across the field bellowing gently, conversationally.

Then he sat down outside the back door and started to chew the cud. Shortly, four of his calves gathered round the remains of the bonfire and sniffed its acrid trails of smoke. The seven cows grazed calmly in a group near the hedge.

They were back.

And settling in.

The first sign had been the clatter of hooves on the road outside. It was an Autumn Sunday evening and we had been resting on the settee in front of a blazing log fire. Out of the window we had seen excited calves leading the way down the hamlet's sloping lane, followed by their mothers — for all the world indulging their children in an escapade. Bringing up the rear was the bull, his flesh rolling with each big stride. He looked like a father who really had something better to do.

The seven calves had spilled through our gateless entrance, trotted across the two-acre field and forced their way out into our neighbour's fallow land through a hole in the hedge. The cows and bull had followed them slowly, enlarging the hole with their bulk.

A few days later, they all came back — the cows through another gap in our sparse and newly-slashed hedge, the bull and the calves up a grassy footpath beside the eastern boundary of the field. Occasionally the bull stopped to rub his great head against trees along the path. We could see the branches bend under the impact of his horns.

A passing car on the road outside the house frightened the calves, who scattered back down the path and entered the field by jumping over the stone wall near the duck pond.

The bull took no notice. He left the path at its junction with the road and strode slowly towards our entrance, watching his family

1

over the hedge. He came through the gate, supremely confident, a mass of muddy flesh, a healing wound on his shoulder. This time he meant business. They were staying.

We'd watched them from the high granite steps leading up to the back door, then retreated to the safety of the scullery window. The bull was only a few feet away and when I took a photograph he turned to glare towards the sound of the shutter. Then he lay down outside the dining room window and the calves started their bonfire-junkie act over the embers of cleared vegetation.

"No gardening today," said my husband Jack.

How did we find ourselves here, deep in the peaceful *France Profonde*, with a bull, seven cows and seven calves in the back garden and the most wonderful neighbours on earth living just opposite?

It's a long story but first I must say that the house found us. Or at least, Marguerite found us — and she had been dead for nine years.

Chapter One

We'd wanted a house in France for 11 years. It had been a dream fostered by a love of the country initially implanted by my mother, who had lived there when she was young. She taught me French words and expressions at the same time as I absorbed English ones: *le tapis, la porte, la fenêtre, les rideaux, s'il vous plaît, merci, la plume de ma tante,* and our family joke — *toute suite and the tooter the sweeter...*

I thought I could speak French until I went to secondary school and discovered she hadn't done verbs.

I learned enough of the language in the formal grammar school way to pass my GCE and promptly forgot most of it when I left school. I became a journalist, married Jack and we had two sons. In the 70s you were not expected to return to work when your children were small, so I stayed at home: writing, designing and printing. Then in 1980 I went back to fulltime journalism. But I never stopped being fascinated by France.

In 1983, as soon as we could afford it, we had our first French holiday. We went with a camping company and stayed in the Loire, the Dordogne and Brittany. All three venues were to have a profound effect on our lives.

We chose Saumur on the Loire because that was where Mother had lived for a year with her best friend, Helen, as the paying guests of a notable local family who were down on their luck. They had lost their *château* and land because of a swindling estate manager and had moved to an elegant house in the town centre where Madame Chevalier, by now widowed, vented her bitterness on all around. The girls moved in fashionable circles, with tea at the Consulate and flirtations with the famous Cadets from the Cavalry School. The household had a maid who by all accounts never washed, and Madame wore the same black clothes every day topped by a choker which hid the wrinkles in her neck and made her feel fashionable again. Mother despised her then but, 70 years later, feels sorry for her — a *grande dame* whose society friends laughed at her predicament, forced to rely on the

Mother could see the four-turreted château from her window.

income from insubordinate English teenagers.

Helen married the son of the family. She was the daughter of an English headmaster and not at all the moneyed catch that Madame had relied upon to restore the family fortunes. Madame was not kind to her and Mother backed her friend stoutly, returning to France to help when her babies were born and when she needed support. She worried all through the War that Helen would be betrayed to the Germans, but she never was. Then she died suddenly of a brain haemorrhage in the early 1950s and her husband died from grief a year later.

The children, who had adored my mother, still think of her as their "second mother" and look upon me and Jack as their English cousins.

It was important for me to find my mother's old haunts in Saumur. My bedroom walls had been covered with 1920s *passe partout* pictures of Cadets on rearing chargers and I had spent the Sunday mornings of my childhood going through her photograph albums so the Consul's garden was as familiar as my own.

The Chevalier house which stood beside the beautiful bridge over the Loire had been destroyed in the war, when the Cavalry School Cadets famously held out against the advancing German army. The family had moved away long before then. The site was still intact and the modern shop which replaced the house was faithful to its former 19th century proportions. I could look across the river at it and imagine my mother there.

But the magnificent four-turreted *château* which Mother could see from her bedroom window remained, now restored and open to the public. The Cavalry School still dominated the town, and the army horses could be seen in neat rows looking out of their stables or on their way to the indoor riding school. Now, however, the Cavalry had some reinforcements: it seemed there were as many tanks at Saumur as horses.

I found the spot on the banks of the river where Mother used to watch the washerwomen and I revelled in the splendid pedestrianisation of the town centre.

And we found the Chevalier family *château* a few kilometres away, built into the side of the hill, where Marguerite of Anjou

5

and Queen of England had died in 1482.

I had a tremendous feeling of oneness with my mother at Saumur and formed a deep attachment to the place. Initially, I wanted to live there myself if we ever had the means.

From Saumur we went to a camp-site near Sarlat, set on the banks of the River Vezère. It was here that our two sons, Alex and Chris (then aged 12 and 13) had their first experience in a canoe. They loved it so much that afterwards they joined a newly-formed canoe club at home and we spent the next five years totally engrossed, supporting their passion for slalom canoeing. It kept us together as a family at a time when many children grow away from their parents and cemented us as the loving unit we are now that they are grown up.

After ten days in the Dordogne we went to a site at the seaside town of Pornic in Southern Brittany. The object was to be near our eldest "French cousin" Annette, who lived in Nantes with her six children.

She showed us the coast and the glamorous resort of La Baule. She drove us at top speed around the city of Nantes, ignoring red traffic lights as she concentrated on speaking English again. (That journey will be etched on our minds for the frantic shouts of *"C'est rouge, Maman!"* from a horrified daughter in the back of the car, each time we came to a lights-controlled road junction and had to swerve to avoid oncoming vehicles). We saw the walled town of Guérande and drove round the salt pans of the *marais*.

But best of all Annette took us home to stay at her flat and to visit her prefabricated "house in the country" which she and her late husband had built from nothing. We learned how to open folding metal shutters, to drink breakfast chocolate from a bowl and to eat croissants. Our "relations" from three generations converged to give us an overwhelming welcome. We became part of French family life for an unforgettable two days. Now we knew two vital things: we loved France and we didn't want to be tourists.

We deliberately tried a different region every year, to see which we liked best. We had fantasies about buying a house, which we thought would never be fulfilled — but it was fun to pretend to be prospective househunters. As we drove hundreds of miles across the country, we idly looked for our ideal style of architecture and our favourite scenery. We still loved Saumur but found the flat countryside around it rather uninspiring. We went to Brittany, the Jura, the Tarn, the Ardêche, the Cote d'Azur, the Pyrénées — almost everywhere except the North East and the Languedoc.

After our first taste of the country, we returned to France every year and built up friendships through various municipal twinning arrangements. Soon we had close friends in the village of Mornant near Lyon, and the towns of Mâcon and Dole. We fostered the links with our "French family" and dropped into the habit of dividing our annual fortnight's holiday by spending a week with friends and a week in a rented house somewhere.

In 1992 we chose the Limousin almost by a process of elimination: we hadn't tried the Centre of France and we liked the photograph of the neat stone house in the brochure. It was love at first sight. We stayed about 20 kilometres South of Limoges in a tiny hamlet with a wonderful panoramic view. It was reached down a leafy lane with small fields on each side, dotted with cows, calves and sheep. There was a forest a few hundred metres away. The old couple who were responsible for the house in the owner's absence were kind and welcoming.

The house itself, though beautifully renovated externally, was the least luxurious we'd hired. We had access to only half of it and were faced with numerous locked doors. We wondered what was behind them — arms caches for the Limousin Liberation Front, perhaps? Elegant rooms full of valuable furniture rather than the 1930s monstrosities in our part? The bed in our room had a convex mattress and we spent all night trying not to roll off. The weather, too, was not kind. It poured every day so we did most of our sightseeing through a blur of raindrops and we video-ed spectacular thunderstorms at night. We made the mistake of doing a load of laundry in the washing machine which then took four days to dry.

Yet none of this mattered. We felt at home in the region as we never had before. We had admired all our past holiday haunts but

7

this one absorbed us and we no longer felt like visitors. We loved the small scale and green colours of the landscape: so much of France was too vast, too barren or too mountainous for us to feel at ease in the longterm. This was hilly, wooded and in many ways reminiscent of our own Cheshire surroundings. The climate was more gentle than the searing heat of the South and warmer than the near-British North.

Following a road at random during a rainy afternoon drive, we stumbled upon a village which took our breath away. Ségur le Château stands on the banks of a curve in the Auvèzere river, overlooked by the ruins of a 12th century castle. The backs of the old houses rise up out of the river and as we parked to watch, swallows were skimming the surface of the fast-flowing water to catch insects. We were captivated by the beauty and timeless quality of the place.

Between showers we went to Oradour-sur-Glane, whose inhabitants were brutally massacred by the Nazis in June 1944 before the village was set on fire. The whole site is a national monument, lovingly maintained in its ruined state and profoundly moving to explore. Fifty years later only the metal objects have survived and almost every house has the skeletons of a bicycle, a Singer sewing machine and a bedstead amid its scorched stones. Visitors (one could almost call them pilgrims) speak in whispers and the overwhelming sound is of birdsong. It's an appalling reminder of the savagery of which the human race is capable. The experience haunted us — for days we could think of nothing else — and cemented us even deeper in our emotional attachment to the Limousin.

We returned to England knowing that we'd found the place where we wanted to plant our roots, but having no idea when or if it would be possible.

In early 1994 we had some astounding news from a solicitor in our home town in Lincolnshire. We learned that Jack, his mother and our sons were among the residuary legatees of Jack's much-loved second cousin Joyce. She had been instrumental in us meeting as a 14-year-old schoolgirl and 18-year-old sixth former when we both helped at her riding school, and she told my anxious mother that "Jack would do for Anne to practise on". We were engaged when I was 18 and married four days after my 21st birthday. We celebrated our silver wedding in 1994.

Joyce was wealthy and shrewd, although she always lived frugally. A true eccentric, she loved to make-do-and-mend, to buy second-hand bargains, to repair equipment until it disintegrated and to hold things together with baler twine. Her kindness to others was legendary and her generosity had always enabled Jack to do things that would otherwise have been out of his reach. His parents had separated during the war and his mother had struggled along fiercely on a tiny income. Joyce had provided opportunities to use his budding DIY skills building her stables, clearing her land and fencing her fields. When he showed an aptitude for dinghy sailing she "bought herself" a racing dinghy, built to Jack's specifications, and said he could have it on permanent loan provided she had one outing a year. She gave me unlimited riding on her ponies for a flat rate of five shillings a week on condition that I helped teach the other riders. Never married, she gave her time unstintingly to her ponies, dogs and other people's children. She was generous with gifts to our family each Christmas and our sons always kept in touch. As she grew older and more eccentric the stench in her house of dogs and steaming saucepans of indescribable dog meat were a penance endured gladly in order to enjoy her company. We were pleased that just before she died of cancer in 1993 we were able to visit her in hospital and thank her for the enormous influence she'd had on our lives. It had never occurred to us that she might leave us anything more than a few hundred pounds.

When we found out about the considerable size of the legacy we knew exactly what she'd want us to do with it. It wasn't destined for the building society or stocks and shares — it was to be spent adventurously on a project that would expand our horizons yet again. An old house in the Limousin would be her monument, and at least half the fun would be the DIY we would need to do to renovate it. It would be sacrilege to put Joyce's money into a neat little ready-made apartment or maisonette. Work, sweat and muddy boots would be essential.

For the past two or three years we had been subscribing to *Living France* magazine. Each month we'd examine the house advertisements minutely, fantasise and choose our favourite property. In the beginning the magazine was crammed with ads for homes to renovate from about £12,000, and we dreamed of buying a farmhouse with a couple of acres for about £15,000. As time went on, the prices went up and the number of properties on offer came down, but our monthly trawl through the ads was a much enjoyed ritual. We kept the magazines in the bathroom and read through them daily at times of contemplation. Our stone-built "fantasy home" had a wood, a stream, a barn, an attic and a cellar. (In our wildest dreams it was a picturesque water mill, in need of loving care, where Jack could play with the millstream and generate electricity). It was in an unspoilt hamlet and there were no other English people for miles around. It was habitable, but we were happy to start off in primitive conditions. We knew this was an impossible quest but we told ourselves to aim high and compromise later.

We promptly booked a *gîte* for two weeks in June in an unfamiliar part of the Limousin, to the East of Limoges, to act as a base for househunting. Chris and his girlfriend Linda agreed to come too. They were electronic engineering students on a year "out" in industry and both loved France.

In April Jack and I started our campaign in earnest. We wrote to all the English and French estate agents in *Living France* who covered the Limousin and also ventured over the border into Allier, where the prices were dearer but there seemed to be more properties available. We described our "fantasy house" and gave a price limit of £20,000, which was within the amount of the expected legacy. We faxed those who gave their fax numbers and then sat back to wait for replies.

Nothing happened for about three weeks and we got tetchy. Then there was great excitement one Saturday morning when the first faxed answer came back. Other replies flowed in and we spent hours hunched over the Michelin map with a magnifying glass trying to find the hamlets where the various properties were situated. We soon found that our fantasy house did not exist, at least not in our stated price range. The more snooty agents said as much and politely ridiculed all suggestions of a watermill.

In lieu of being able to do something decisive, we filled the hours of anticipation by creating charts specifying the attributes of each property we liked, and adding questions that needed to be answered. Has this house got a septic tank? Does that one have a pond? Is the roof really sound or is an optical illusion? We pounced on every detail in the descriptions, comparing each *"fermette* suitable for renovation" with its rivals. The fat file with its neat transparent punched pockets filled with photocopied particulars became a vital document.

We discounted the homes in the Allier as too expensive and were relieved to find that prices in the Limousin seemed to be lower than anywhere else in France. We hadn't deliberately plumped for the cheapest area, but it was a bonus, even if our ideal home was elusive.

We sent for books on buying and renovating a house in France and taught ourselves all about the French system of selling property, which uses an impartial government lawyer (*notaire*) to draw up the agreements. We learned about moving money to France and opening a bank account. We re-read our stack of *Living France* magazines for snippets of information we'd missed when the dream was just a dream.

Then we saw an advertisement for a French property exhibition at Harrogate in a couple of days' time and managed to book places at the seminars on house renovation and the legalities of buying a home in France.

The exhibition was exciting because we were suddenly surrounded by likeminded people who had either done what we intended to do or were equally determined to. It no longer seemed a sort of private perversion pursued behind closed doors. We were suddenly putting our names on lists and telling agents that we were going to the Limousin for two weeks in June to buy a house. We were allowing a week for looking and a week for signing the first contract. The professionals didn't seem to think we were crazy.

The legal expert, however, did. His first words in his seminar were: "If you are thinking of buying a house in France, my advice is DON'T." His audience gasped. We were not sure if he was having a bad day (it was the umpteenth day of the travelling exhibition and he'd already done the talk repeatedly) or being horribly honest. He advised renting first in the area where you wanted to live, so that you could pick and choose among the available properties and make sure you knew the district — sensible advice, but we couldn't follow it. We simply didn't have the time. He made the legal transaction sound like a minefield.

"Many English people buying property in France leave their brains behind in Dover," he added and told us some disaster stories. "Don't go to a *notaire* whose documents are typed out on an ancient typewriter in an old-fashioned office," he warned. "He will probably have spent the afternoon playing golf with the vendor and won't do you any favours." It was all a sobering antidote to the earlier euphoria and probably very necessary.

We recognised one of the agencies who had been slow to reply to our correspondence and arranged to see three of their properties on the Tuesday of our first week in June. We also made a rendezvous with another agent who specialised in the Limousin but did not advertise in *Living France*.

Now all our househunting days were accounted for and we just had to contain our mounting excitement as June approached. We'd worked out a list of 20 houses we wanted to see and had graded them in desirability according to their photographs and descriptions. We could repeat parrot-fashion everything the agents had cared to write about them. We were ready to get Grade A in Advanced Level House-buying. Only time would tell if the cramming had been worth it.

Chapter Two

 W e were looking for good omens en route to the Limousin in June and we played a game we'd read about in *France* magazine, whose readers had been carrying on a fascinating correspondence in the letters columns on the virtues of Norbert-spotting.

A "Norbert" we learned was a Norbert Dentressangle truck in easily identifiable red and white livery, the N and D joined together in one flowing logo. Fans broke the tedium of long journeys by counting them, giving themselves points for special cases (loading behind one in the ferry was especially pointsworthy) and even photographing them after spectacular mishaps. Readers who managed to snap a picture of a Norbert driver (known as a *Norbeur*) carrying a copy of *France* magazine could earn a bottle of champagne.

We thought if ever we needed a good Norbert count it was now. A gratifying Norbert score under our belts would be like walking down a long pavement without stepping on the cracks. It would just have to point to happy househunting.

Chris and Linda, veterans of long family car journeys, joined in the game like naturals.

The Norberts were shy from Cheshire to Portsmouth. We saw about five — average for the trip. We sailed overnight to Caen and remained in Normandy the next day looking at the preparations for the D-Day 50th anniversary celebrations which would follow shortly. We stayed at one of our favourite *chambres d'hôte* farmhouses near Argentan. We were exploring off the Norbert track and didn't expect to do well.

But once we set off in the morning they came out *en masse*. Every Norbert driver in France must have decided to cross our path. We counted 51: a phenomenal score. With a count like that, Fate must be smiling on us, we decided.

We were bursting to show Chris and Linda our wonderful Limousin, but as anxious as new suitors in case they didn't approve. Linda had lived in France; Chris had been with us to

The first house we viewed was the unfinished bargain.

many parts — but neither had visited this region. They were currently working for Michelin at Stoke-on-Trent, only half an hour from our Cheshire home. There had been massive redundancies at the factory and they were not particularly happy. Michelin's headquarters were in Clermont-Ferrand and as we got further South there were more signs to Clermont at the major road junctions. They referred to it, with a shudder, as "the C-F word."

The scenery began to change from flat agricultural plains to a more intimate landscape. We came over the border into the Berry and felt we were almost home, then crossed into the Limousin with hearts racing. Was it still OK? Did we still like it? Had we made the right decision?

Yes, we had. This new part of the region was as beautiful as the haunts we had explored two years before. The love affair was still on.

The *gîte* where we were staying was in a tiny hamlet near St Leonard-de-Noblat. It was a renovated stone house which had been doubled in size by extending into the attached barn. Inside the house, and from the outside, it was an integrated whole. Inside the barn we could see the breeze block structure of the extension, which filled only part of the building. It seemed strange to us but we came across many other extensions done this way, to comply with French planning laws.

The *gîte* was owned by a wonderful family. I had mentioned in letters that we were going to use it while we looked for a house of our own and the family could not have been more helpful. In advance they gave us cuttings from the property sections of the local newspapers, and after we arrived they advised us on the best *notaire* and even found us a house in the country which had been repossessed and was about to be auctioned. They expected it would go for a bargain price. Sadly, it wasn't at all what we were looking for, but we appreciated their efforts.

Our first estate agent's appointment was in Uzerche at 9.30am. We had as always underestimated the distance and the time it would take to get there. In England on the map it looked a straightforward journey but judging by the time it had taken to cover similar distances on the way down, we decided we needed to allow at least an hour and a half. It seemed strange to set the alarm clock for 7am when we were supposed to be on holiday, though I was so excited that I could hardly sleep. These five houses were the best of the bunch and we would measure the rest against them.

When we set off we were armed with a hand-held halogen light so that we could examine dark corners and a video camera so that we could record each house. We knew that with 20 houses to see, one would soon begin to merge into another. We also followed the advice we'd read in an excellent book by J Kater Pollock about buying property in France and took boiler suits, heavy boots, a hard hat, our file of information about the houses, a small electrical screwdriver for poking suspected patches of dry rot, binoculars for inspecting roofs and a compass. Jack had been a Queen's Scout and "Be prepared!" was our motto.

You buy without a professional survey in France and we were determined to spot any major defects in the properties we were going to view.

The agent was a woman who spoke English very well. We always try to be polite and speak French when in France but her English was so superior to our French that we were relieved to give up the unequal struggle.

We sat in her attractively-renovated office and went through the familiar list of properties we had earmarked. One was sold. Two she dismissed at once.

"No — I could not take anyone there. The house is filthy and the kitchen is full of chickens. You would not like that one. And this house — on the photograph it has many oak trees. I managed to get the brothers who own it to agree the price. That was very difficult. Then when I visited it the next time one of them had cut down the oak trees. He has ruined it and I am very angry."

She was a strong character. We got the impression she could hardly bring herself to sell certain houses. We insisted on going to one that she was reluctant to show us: Jack was drawn to the fact that it had an old pond and he couldn't tell from the photograph whether it was picturesquely rundown or on the verge of falling down. It was also very cheap.

Another property was our mystery gamble: she was happy to take us to see a large unfinished house with a lot of land at a ridiculous bargain price. She chucked in a couple of her own suggestions for viewing which looked interesting from their photographs and was pleased to confirm that our very favourite prospect was still on the market. This added up to a morning's whirlwind tour of five houses in a 20km radius of her office.

We split into two cars. I travelled with her and Jack drove behind with Chris and Linda; some way behind, in fact. The problem was that she knew where she was going and he didn't. She knew she could approach the blind bends at 60mph and live to tell the tale (perhaps) but he wasn't about to take her word for it.

"I do find that English men drive so slowly," she observed, accelerator to the carpet.

The first house we viewed was the unfinished bargain. On the way she explained that it had been built 30 years previously for a bachelor who had hoped to get married. His plans had fallen through so he had sensibly stopped the building, living only in the parts he needed. The isolated house had white rendered walls and a slate roof, and consisted of a large garage at basement level, a kitchen, a bathroom and a bedroom — and lots of space. All the materials to finish it off were there, in bags and plastic wrapping. The old man had died at the age of about 80 and the property was being sold by his relatives who had inherited it.

From the garden it appeared to be an outdoor fridge museum. He might have had no mod. cons. inside but there were at least four or five fridges in the overgrown garden. We climbed the outside steps to the front door, determined to keep open minds. We had, after all, wanted to do a spot of serious DIY.

The kitchen was, well, a kitchen. Anyway, it had a stainless steel sink. It was about as clean as you would expect an 80-year-old bachelor to leave it. Off this room was a lavatory and next to that a shower room. We noted that after 30 years the labels were still stuck on the pristine sanitaryware. It looked as if he hadn't gone in much for actually using such fripperies. The bedroom, presumably designed as a dining room, had an oak parquet floor.

And that was it!

The agent opened another door which led into a large unplastered area filled with building materials. It covered the rest of the first floor. We poked at the packaging: parquet blocks, an oak front door, copper pipes, plumbing and electrical requisites, rolls of fibreglass insulation, a bidet and another lavatory bowl. Everywhere was dusty but the materials themselves were in very good condition. French windows opened on to an unguarded balcony.

She led us to another part of the house, up a rudimentary staircase, then warned us to be careful. A few planks ran from joist to joist, otherwise it was a vast open space just waiting to be filled in, lit by dormer windows. The walls were of the characteristic red hollow bricks, hung with cobwebs.

It certainly had, er, possibilities.

Down in the basement garage there were bags of solid 30-year-old plaster everywhere, plus lots more materials. There was also the detritus of the old man's life, including several rusty bicycles, two wheelbarrows, gas bottles, stacked planks and a lot of empty wooden barrels. Some climbing and squeezing enabled us to clamber into a wine cellar.

It would have taken a week just to clear it all out.

Another big room on the same level, reached from the outside, contained an interesting mixture of ancient and modern: a wooden hand-driven grain mill, old farm implements, the beginnings of a central heating system and metal shutters still in their packaging.

There was a rotovator-type plough parked under a sheet by the house.

The land, which was a strange shape, included fruit trees, a field and some woods. It totalled about 16 acres. We were intrigued. In our minds' eye we could see the finished project. As a family we had the skills to do the job, we had the tools and we had the materials. Would we have the time or the patience? We had set our hearts on an old house, but this new one was soundly constructed and would not need any repair work. It would certainly be a challenge. And it was half the price the finished house would be worth.

A few hair-raising kilometres away we found the second property, which had not been on our original list. It was old, built in the local style of a low house with attached barn. There was a small garden, outbuildings and a spring which gushed out of a tap into a trough. The owner had started to renovate it but had been taken ill. It was deceptive: not all the buildings on the site were for sale and in the house itself the small rooms felt oppressive. The floors were very uneven and it was damp in places. There were some major cracks which went all the way through the walls and a hole in the attic floor. Some of the roof timbers were rotten and others were sprouting a white fungus. Most of the outbuildings had corrugated iron roofs, though the house itself was tiled. The only attractive feature was a stone balcony off one of the bedroom windows. The price was the same as for the unfinished house. We weren't drawn to it at all and didn't stay long.

The third house was also a last-minute suggestion. It had beautiful barns and an attractive site with a vegetable garden and fruit trees as well as its own spring water. The outbuildings included stables and rabbit hutches. It was tempting until we went into the house, which had belonged to the vendor's grandparents. Once again this was dark, dirty, depressing — and full of junk. I couldn't imagine anyone living there during the 20th century. Cleaning it would have required some advice from Hercules. Like the other house, there was a kitchen, two other rooms downstairs, two small bedrooms and a roof space (complete with old leather saddle) which could be converted. And that was it.

"Even Victorian terraced houses had a privy," I thought.

"I know this seems a very naive question," I said to the estate agent, "but what did the people in all these houses do about going to the lavatory?"

"Oh, I expect they went in the barn with the animals," she replied matter-of-factly.

The fourth house was the cheap one she didn't want to show us. We soon found out why. It wasn't that the particulars were misleading, they were just erring a tiny bit on the positive side...

It had been empty for so long that a large tree had grown in the middle of the approach road. The "old pond" was a dry indentation in the ground. The land was part overgrown and part cultivated by a neighbour, so dreams of a snug little home in a wood were out. The barns, which were also being used by the neighbour, were well-tended, newly-roofed and in very good condition. The house had a new roof too, but was otherwise nearly derelict. The interior looked as if it had been gutted by fire, it was so black and disgusting. There was a hole in the ceiling. Old wallpaper, darkened by damp, scrolled limply from the walls. In other rooms the plaster had fallen off. It theoretically had electricity and old wiring dangled from the black ceiling roses. The place made our flesh creep. The only way to renovate it would have been to knock it down and start again.

The fifth house was the one we'd selected from the agent's particulars as being the most promising. It was on the outskirts of a village, whereas the others were isolated. It had good accommodation and a reasonable amount of land. It was also by far the most expensive.

We got lost *en route*, which made Jack's journey all the more confusing. I was enjoying the agent's company and had long reconciled myself to sitting with clenched buttocks.

When we arrived we were relieved to find that the house fitted the description and was habitable. It was a holiday home which belonged to a couple who were divorcing and wanted to sell. It consisted of two houses knocked together, one much smaller and lower than the other. The inside was clean but not inspiring and owners' renovations had been rudimentary. It too had wonderful barns: one with a resident barn owl which we saw flying around in the rafters. A spring came up through a tap, filled a horse-trough and then bubbled along the boundary with a pretty, timeless sound. Most of the land was up to the side of the buildings and there was also an orchard across a public path. It was the best old property we'd seen, but...

What about the lavatory? The slope of the land was all wrong to install a septic tank. Would the land above the house be a disadvantage? You certainly had to climb up to it and couldn't enjoy looking at it from the house. Would the footpath be fraught with legal problems? Was it worth the high price? Did we want to live in such a big village?

Driving back to the gîte we were crestfallen to find that none of the old houses had fired our imaginations. In fact most of them had revolted us, if we were strictly honest. Were we coming all the way to France to renovate a 1960s house without any of the romantic extras we'd hoped for? Was it all going to go wrong? We did not hold out any hopes for our next day's viewing with the first agency we'd talked to at the French property exhibition, whose houses were way down our list of priorities. If the best houses were so awful, where would their less promising ones be on the scale?

Tuesday's viewing was with a French estate agency in Limoges which acted for the British company. We'd made our appointment for 10am and arrived a few minutes early. We explained ourselves in French to the people sharing the main office and they directed us to a connecting office to wait for our English-speaking contact. At about 10.15am a little Irishman turned up. He checked what we wanted and we had a sneaking suspicion that this was the first thought he'd given us. It was all in marked contrast to the day before.

We repeated: we wanted a house to renovate, which wasn't a ruin. We wanted to be able to at least "camp" in it while we worked. We wanted somewhere in the country, with no less than an acre of land, with outbuildings and some sort of water feature like a stream or a pond. We didn't mind installing a septic tank, but we wanted water and electricity to be connected already — new connections to such public utilities could be very expensive. And we simply couldn't afford to pay more than 250,000FF for the whole transaction — 225,000FF would be more comfortable for the bank balance.

We showed him the particulars which we had received from the English agents. Two of the three houses were already sold. The third had a picture and specifications which — in the light of the previous day's experiences — could have spelled a delightful place or somewhere not worth visiting. He consulted his files.

21

This farmhouse was on the books of a *notaire* in a town 50 kilometres away: we would go and get the keys.

Jack drove and the little agent chattered. He was delightful, very friendly and full of the blarney. We thought we probably couldn't trust him an inch, but we wanted to. He was a nice person to be manipulated by. Chris and Linda privately dubbed him "the Leprechaun."

We arrived at the *notaire's* office. It was modern, attractive and had a hum of efficiency. Worthy posters plastered the walls of the waiting area. Jack approved of their computers.

The staff didn't recognise the particulars of the house and they certainly hadn't got the keys. We were ready to write off the day as a waste of time. We had other people to see later in the week and the property in question was about 19th on the list of 20. It didn't matter, we said.

Embarrassed, they asked us to look through their books to see if there was anything else we fancied. Jack and the others had lost interest by now, so I leafed through the albums and chose a few properties which were the right price and had some land. I mistakenly picked up a book of houses outside our price range and spotted an ugly ivy-covered house with an overgrown garden which was described as having two acres of land and added it in for luck. It was far too expensive, 285,000FF, but the Leprechaun said that wasn't significant. "All prices are negotiable," was his motto.

I discovered that this house was the furthest away. The keys were at the *notaire's* branch office in another town. Private tutting noises went on in the office. I said I'd only selected it at random and wouldn't mind at all if we didn't see it. Politely, with fixed smiles, they insisted that *madame* should see it if she wanted to... Arrangements were made for us to pick up these keys and the Leprechaun pocketed the others.

The weather was gorgeous — a hot, sunny day. It was almost too hot to be stuck five in a car on a wild goose chase.

We drove off on a convoluted journey, the Leprechaun navigating. We found the other *notaire's* office and collected the keys. It was about 12.30pm and we were keen to do something, *anything*, constructive. We'd used up an entire morning without seeing a single building.

So the Leprechaun saw a restaurant and said it was time for lunch. He said he'd pay, which made it more bearable. We were, after all, using our own petrol for the whole escapade. It was a leisurely lunch, typically good: the sort promised in books about France. The sort you never find yourself. The sort you wouldn't mind replacing with a quick ham sandwich when you are in a hurry.

It was nearly 2pm when we set out on the trail of the ivy covered house which we felt morally bound to visit. It was in a dot on the map called St Paradis. We drove through St Paradis and there was nothing remotely resembling the photograph. The only property for sale was a beautiful double-fronted granite house with a massive attached barn, which dominated the centre of the village. It had a rampant vine growing over the front and led straight out on to the lane. There was no sign of any ivy or an overgrown garden. The barn was on the wrong side, too.

The Leprechaun jumped out and spoke to an elderly couple who were standing on the doorstep of their nearby home. They shook their heads. There was only one house in the village for sale and it was the one we could see. It had been empty for years. Then the old man had a brainwave — perhaps the photograph had been taken from the back?

The Leprechaun explained about his English clients and the wife said: "We do hope they will buy it and repopulate the village." We were enchanted. Even if it wasn't the right house, such a welcome was heartwarming. We had been so afraid that foreign homeowners would be as unpopular in France as they were in North Wales.

We parked the car and walked round the back of the buildings into a big field. There had been a lot of rain and our shoes sank into the mud in spite of the bright sunshine which made everywhere look so attractive. And there it was — the plain building covered with ivy, a jungle of brambles bounded by barbed wire separating the house from the field. We were stunned that anyone wanting to sell the place could be so stupid as to neglect the elegant facade and use this rear view on a brochure.

The front door was of carved oak. The key was enormous and looked more suitable for a bank vault. After a struggle the Leprechaun managed to get it to turn. He immediately dashed round opening the shutters and letting in the rays of the sun.

The front door led straight into a big kitchen, which had a traditional smoke-blackened Limousin fireplace or *cantou* with a high mantelpiece and iron hook to hang a cooking pot over the fire. There was a shallow white porcelain sink with a single cold tap and a cupboard in the wall by the fire. The walls were white at the top and grey at the bottom and the floor was some kind of concrete patterned with a design. The oak-beamed ceiling was high and there were books and old newspapers scattered on the floor. It felt spacious and habitable.

A door at the back led to a smaller room. It had been divided off by a modern concrete wall to create a very basic toilet. The wall had had a skim of plaster and a lick of paint but the door and door-frame were unpainted. The lavatory looked as if it had hardly been used.

The Leprechaun had found it impossible to open the shutters in this back room. Ivy and brambles had grown through the ventilating louvres and enmeshed them tightly closed.

We went back into the kitchen. The stairs led off from a brown-painted door and turned a right angle against the back wall of the house. There was no handrail. They were very old and the wall looked very old, too. While the other walls had been plastered flat, this was lumpy as though the stones had been covered crudely with lime. At the top of the stairs was a tiny window half-filled with rusty gauze, which seemed to let the house breathe. Everywhere the floorboards were of solid oak, about nine inches wide.

"This could be your bathroom," said the Leprechaun in a small room off the landing, about 6ft x 9ft. The wall around the window was disfigured with damp and the stone frame of the window was in a poor shape in places, but it was nothing in comparison with what we'd seen the day before.

Like the kitchen, the room was decorated in a two-tone colour scheme. The top two thirds of the walls were pink and the bottom third was a much darker shade. One wall had been scratched back to the plaster at waist-height, presumably by a bed-head or perhaps even a tin bath, and the ceiling had been boxed in to hide the beams. The panelled door was green — and filthy.

The next room off the landing was an enormous bedroom. It was over the kitchen and the same size. It had retained its beams and there were two windows looking out into the street but obscured by leaves and branches of the vine which climbed over the facade. It had a fireplace with a wooden surround and was painted white. There were a few superficial cracks in the plaster but nothing serious. The green door was the same design as the other and equally grimy. But the sun was shining straight in and it was possible to ignore the cobwebs and imagine the room in its heyday.

Past the wooden steps to the attic was a bedroom about 9ft x 12ft with faded red wallpaper and a once-pretty border. The window looked out across the field but the panes were half-covered with ivy. Another door led from here into what must have been the most attractive room of all, measuring 12ft x 18ft and papered in pale green with matching borders top and bottom. The paper had yellowed but it was possible to see that it must have been chosen with great care and put on professionally in the days before butt-joints. The room boasted a fireplace with an ebony-effect wooden surround and the marks above it suggested that a matching mirror had hung there once. From the window we could see up the street but once again the view was obscured by the vine. The beams in these interconnecting rooms had all been boxed in and in each ceiling, poking through a hole in the plasterboard, hung a light switch of the sort that dangles above a bed. The frayed flexes looked lethal.

We explored the attic using the halogen lamp. It was full of fascinating objects but we were more interested in the structure. The roof and woodwork looked brand new and the stones seemed freshly pointed. Indeed a few wooden plaster mixing containers full of crumbly white lumps had been abandoned there by the workmen. Dormer windows at the front added the final touch.

We went back downstairs to explore another room off the kitchen which we'd missed first time round. The door caught on the uneven floorboards and we threw ourselves against it. The room we discovered ran the whole depth of the house, measuring about 13ft x 27ft. It had a window at the back, criss-crossed with brambles, and a door out into the road. There was a fireplace with a wooden surround but the place looked more like a workshop than a dining room. The floorboards were spongy and broken in places and plaster was coming off the walls. To be frank, it was awful.

In the floor there was a trapdoor to the cellar, which was reached by a set of stone steps. Jack and Chris ventured down with the lamp and reported that part of it appeared to have been hewn out of the granite on which the house was built. It was ventilated by a gauze-covered window at the back and the stone floor felt as if it was covered with a carpet of rotted wood. It was impossible to stand upright but otherwise it wasn't unpleasant.

The barn was the next area to be inspected. It was divided into three with mangers and haylofts along each side and a high unrestricted part in the middle reached by an enormous door. It was full of straw and hay and smelled lovely. It exuded peace — I could have stayed all afternoon.

We squelched up and down the field, finding there was a very marshy part. Cattle had been grazing on the pasture and their feet had sunk deep into the mud, creating ankle-breaking holes.

Our presence had been noted by other curious villagers. One elderly woman told us that when she was a child it had been her job to take cheeses from the village dairy down into the cellar of the house. She had always been frightened.

She showed us the village well on the border of the property, topped by a tiny shrine, and pointed to where a small stream filled a former pond in the field. We found a deep well belonging to the house near the entrance to the field.

Another woman said that the house had belonged to a couple whose only son had disappeared in the war. The husband had died first, and then the widow, Marguerite. The house had been shuttered and empty for years but it had obviously once been loved and cared for.

I found myself clasping the neighbours' hands and telling them: "This is a wonderful house and we would love to buy it. I hope to see you again very soon, Madame." And they each replied, "Yes, I hope so too." Yet we had not discussed it as a family and it was much too expensive. The house had drawn us to itself from nowhere and pulled us tightly to its bosom. I wanted it so much that I felt sick and weak. I was in the throes of falling in love with St Paradis. So was Linda.

The Leprechaun dismissed the price problem. "You always expect to knock off a bit," he said. "Everything is negotiable. Don't worry about it."

We forced ourselves to curb our enthusiasm and look at the other houses on the list that day. They might be even better.

The next was very hard to find. When we eventually tracked down the village the people were not forthcoming or welcoming. They pointed it out reluctantly and said they thought it was already sold to a hairdresser.

We eventually found the red brick house behind a high cover of trees and shrubs. It was cheaper than St Paradis but had few of its attributes and we looked at it politely but without real interest. We were mildly surprised to find that one room downstairs was like the *Marie Celeste*: it appeared that the builders had just downed tools and run away without finishing the conversion.

We wandered round upstairs and noted some big cracks. A mattress in one of the bedrooms also appeared to have been abandoned. We came downstairs and noticed that a wall had been knocked out between the kitchen and dining room and a wooden support put in to replace it. Just as Chris and Jack spotted that the support was bowed and under incredible pressure, I followed a hunch and ran outside to check something. Yes — the cracks extended inside and out. Yes — the front of the house was falling out. Yes — they had taken down a load-bearing wall. We imagined the panic when the building started to disintegrate with a loud crack and we visualised the builders running for their lives. We thought of the poor hairdresser and concluded that he should have stuck to shampooing.

Back in England, we found the intact house featured in an old edition of *Living France* and grieved for its sad fate. Who'd buy it now?

The next property we went to see was not of our choosing. It was the Leprechaun's idea. He said we wouldn't like the one on the *notaire*'s particulars and he'd got something much more to our taste. I took it with a pinch of salt, but it was a wonderful day, I was in love and I didn't care if he took us to the monkey house at the zoo.

We drove through the attractive town of Bujaleuf on the banks of the River Maulde which eventually drains into — and out of — the famous Lake Vassivière. It thrives on the holiday trade, with visitors coming to enjoy watersports on the river.

Just outside the town we turned off along a dusty track, parked the car and walked down to a stone farm with barns and outbuildings. The view was outstanding. The farm had a lot of land which stretched almost as far as the eye could see, most of it down to hay. The price was much too high. "No problem," said the Leprechaun, "A neighbouring farmer wants to buy some of the land."

It had a wood. It had a stream. It had a beautiful pond full of tiny fish. Jack was in love.

Poor Linda, who suffers from hayfever, was in paroxysms of sneezing as we explored the land in the afternoon sunshine. We went inside while the men admired the fields.

The Leprechaun explained that the house had once been two separate dwellings with a single staircase — a common arrangement when different generations of the same family farmed a single piece of land. The houses were two-up two-down mirror images of each other with small rooms. The elderly owners, who had been persuaded to move away, had had one side extended into the barn and created a large dining room, a bathroom and a separate lavatory.

The attic was spacious and interesting. We found a suspicious large dropping up there that the Leprechaun assured us was only an owl's. We could also see that repointing was pretty necessary.

The owners' belongings were still everywhere, piled up in the rooms. In one bedroom a teddy bear sat bolt upright on a bare mattress. In another the household linen was in neat stacks. It was all so sad. We were told we could have what goods or furniture we wanted — presumably at a price.

I felt quite indifferent about it, except for the bathroom tiles which I knew I couldn't live with. The pond was a great plus factor, as was the stream, the wood and the land, but the farm buildings were being used by a neighbour who presumably would not be thrilled to give up this arrangement, and the hay came right up to the dining room French windows. Would Linda ever be able to come to stay?

Jack and Chris went down into the cellar and were troubled by the dry rot and mould they discovered. But I knew Jack was still in love. Chris, a sensible soul, who didn't give his heart away easily, was just at the stage of fancying both properties equally.

The last house was a disaster. It was built practically into the side of a hill and although it had quite a bit of land in theory, this was useless because it was going up at an angle of about 70°. It had been "done up" on a shoestring by a young French sawmill worker who had tried his best but had just succeeded in making the place look tacky. There was no comparison between what he had to offer and the charms of St Paradis and Bujaleuf, or even the unique challenge of Uzerche.

After we'd dropped off the Leprechaun in Limoges we drove home delighted. We might differ on the choice but we weren't going to get nasty with each other about it. At least there was a genuine choice and we were unlikely to go home without fixing something up which would change our lives for ever.

We thought it wasn't bad going for a day which we'd written off at eleven o'clock in the morning.

As we explored the house we knew it just had to be this one.

Chapter Three

Next day we gave ourselves a break. We didn't think we could impose constant househunting on Chris and Linda. It was strange: the owners of the St Leonard *gîte* had given us the name of their *notaire*, who also sold property, several weeks before we came to France and we had arranged to spend part of the Wednesday with his English employee who dealt with inquiries from British hopefuls. We knew the contact's name but the name of his firm defeated us — there were several partners with long French names. Then the more we thought about it, the more we had the horrible feeling that it was the same *notaire* as we had visited with the Leprechaun. We'd had three whole *départements* to choose from, with literally hundreds of different *notaires*. The coincidence was extraordinary, and embarrassing. A quick check of headed notepaper confirmed the gaffe. We had to ring the Englishman up and say we'd already been through his books and were interested in two of the firm's properties, though we wouldn't know for sure until the end of the week. We thought it wasn't worth going all the way over to the office again and didn't want to waste his time. He wasn't very pleased, muttering dark things about the Leprechaun — presumably seeing his personal commission disappear.

So we decided to forget about houses for a day and go to Futuroscope at Poitiers.

On Thursday we had arranged to see another English agent who had been at the property exhibition in England. We'd taken about 20 of her particulars and sent her a list of the ones we fancied. Again we set off really early in the morning to make the 9.30am appointment. We were going cross country for much of the time and the roads were slow.

It was the old story. The three most promising houses were already spoken for. They'd met all our criteria, so we were disappointed. We chose some more from her books and then she marked a map of the area with the positions of all the properties we wanted to see. She suggested we did our own "recce" and came back the following day with specific ones we really wanted to visit. It would save her time not to accompany us to places we then dismissed out of hand, she argued. We thought it was certainly a novel sort of customer care.

It was hard to find the houses and as the day progressed we realised none of us wanted to. Linda and I were faithful in our love for St Paradis; Jack was still besotted with Bujaleuf. Chris sympathised with both camps and kept his counsel. Uzerche was still a possibility. We were sick of other houses. To force ourselves to visit them and pretend to be interested felt like prostitution. It was as if we'd found a soulmate and then joined a dating agency.

We went home early and rang the agent, saying truthfully that our favourite properties on her list had been sold and we'd found nothing to better the ones we'd viewed earlier in the week. She was probably furious but covered it up.

We put the houses in an unemotional order of merit:

Bujaleuf had wonderful land, a stream and a pond teeming with fish; it had a bathroom, was immediately habitable but needed repointing and a new floor in the kitchen. It was in a holiday area so our friends, relations and future grandchildren would have plenty to do when they came to stay. The downside was that we could not afford all the land and it was isolated.

St Paradis had a wonderful house and poorer quality land. It had a potential pond and a tiny stream. Structurally the house was in excellent condition but it seemed to have become stuck in a timewarp. It was in a hamlet and the neighbours were welcoming. But we suspected that at best the lavatory drained into a cesspit and even if we managed to get the price down we would have no money left over to install a septic tank — for the time being, anyway.

Uzerche was a one-off challenge. All the materials were there to finish it once we'd cleared up the mess. We would double its value. It had lots of land. But it was modern, unromantic, very isolated and two hours' drive further South than the other properties.

We agonised. We watched and re-watched the videos we'd made of the three places. We drove back to Bujaleuf and inspected the site from the top of a nearby hill. We pored over the plans, trying to parcel the land so that we'd get all the interesting bits. It couldn't be done in our price-bracket.

Late on the Friday afternoon we telephoned the Leprechaun and said we would like to see St Paradis and Bujaleuf again. He apologised profusely, Bujaleuf had just been sold to a young farmer, buying with a Government start-up grant, who would keep it all as one holding. The Leprechaun hadn't realised when he took us round that negotiations were going on. We were sorry but pleased. It would have been morally wrong to have chopped up the farm for the sake of making it into a holiday and retirement home.

Jack fell in love with St Paradis on the rebound.

The decision had been made for us: we would go back to St Paradis and if we still loved it we would try to negotiate for it. The owner would surely drop his price a bit.

Next day we met the Leprechaun and apologised for ruining his Saturday afternoon off. It was pouring with rain — much more a normal Limousin climate for us than the wonderful sunshine which had graced the day we first saw St Paradis.

As we explored the house again, we knew it just had to be this one. In spite of the rain and grey skies, the dust and cobwebs, the brambles and ivy, it was beautiful. It was a house with dignity and a proud past which seemed to have been put in mothballs for at least a generation. We would give it a future.

The crowning moment came when Jack and Chris spotted the plastic vent for a septic tank running up the back wall beside the ivy. This meant there was a working lavatory, one cold tap and one electric socket. What more could we ask for?

We'd had part of Joyce's inheritance but there was a legal problem over death duties and the rest was expected any time. Jack's mother had promised to tide us over with a certain sum if we needed the equivalent of a bridging loan until it arrived. This took us to our original target figure we'd given the estate agents. Now Chris said that he would lend us the extra money we needed to buy St Paradis from his own part of the inheritance.

The Leprechaun came home with us and filled in some forms. We said we would offer 265,000FF initially going up to 270,000 if absolutely necessary. We simply could not go any higher. He told us that he had seen some papers at the *notaire*'s which indicated that the first stage of house purchase, the *compromis de vente*, had gone through very recently on St Paradis for 265,000FF and that the seller had then pulled out for some reason. This was most unusual. A *compromis de vente* was rarely rescinded. A reneging seller lost the 10 per cent deposit and had to pay an additional 10 per cent financial penalty; a buyer having second thoughts lost their deposit. It was usually the buyer who dropped out because they could not get planning permission for something they wanted to do. To have a reluctant vendor was very odd. The Leprechaun thought we ought to be OK offering around the same price again, when it had obviously been acceptable before. He would make our offer known first thing on Monday morning. We were leaving the following Saturday morning and hoped to have all the formalities done by then. We had arranged with our bank in England to send money for a deposit over as soon as we alerted them by fax. It was all well-organised in advance and very simple. We expected it all to be in hand by Tuesday.

The owner, we were told, was a distant relation of the widow Marguerite. He lived in Paris and was a retired lawyer.

Then the waiting game started.

Chris and Linda hired a little Twingo car and went off for a mini-holiday of their own in the Dordogne, fingers firmly crossed. Jack and I telephoned the Limoges agency every day. Most of the time the Leprechaun was out with other clients. When we did get him he hadn't heard anything.

I was nearly out of my mind.

Jack handles things more stoically.

I couldn't sleep, could barely eat and could think of nothing else. Jack was going off the Uzerche house on the grounds that it was too isolated and too far to drive. That was the last straw for me. We had lost the farm at Bujaleuf, if we lost St Paradis and he didn't want Uzerche then we would have wasted a fortnight. We hadn't even seriously looked anywhere else. We'd seen St Paradis in another agent's shop window. Had someone else pipped us at the post? I couldn't bear to think about it. All our carefully-timed plans would be thwarted. I thought I was going to die from sheer disappointment.

On the Thursday afternoon Jack and I set off in search of a replacement house. We had cuttings from the local paper, courtesy of our sweet landlady — who was sharing our ups and downs with great empathy — and a publication which showed many local *notaires'* properties for sale. It was no consolation that St Paradis was in there too, photographed from the front.

One place which sounded ideal on paper was almost underneath a main line railway viaduct. The others required patient and inspired map-reading, but yielded little of interest. Our hearts were set on St Paradis and nothing else compared with it, however unemotional and practical we tried to be. We would just have to face being "jilted", go home to England and start all over again in a calm and systematic way. Perhaps we could come back in September, when we'd originally planned to take over our new property. It served us right for being so cocky. We were spectacular failures at A Level Housebuying.

Chris and Linda came back on the Thursday night, shattered to find that nothing at all had happened. We faced with little pleasure the prospect of a dinner the following night to celebrate her 21st birthday and Jack's 50th.

At 10am on Friday the Leprechaun rang to say that our offer of 270,000FF had been turned down. It was 280,000FF (£33,000 at the current exchange rate) or nothing. This was £11,000 more than we expected from Joyce. We knew we'd never find anything better and that the price was fair. We just hadn't got that much. We couldn't ask Chris for any more, he needed the money himself. But Chris insisted that he would lend us whatever was necessary. He and Linda loved St Paradis as much as we did and it was going to be our family house. We hugged him and agreed the price.

Jack and I went to Limoges for 2pm that afternoon. By 4pm the *compromis de vente* was signed on our part and the money had been faxed. We agreed that the Leprechaun would act as our proxy when the final *acte de vente* was signed six weeks later. We went with the Leprechaun to the city branch of the Societé

Générale bank and with his help opened an account in the nearest big town to St Paradis.

Another two hours and it would have been too late. We could breathe again. The joint birthday dinner at a nearby hotel over-looking the river was a great success. Chris had bought Linda a diamond ring — not an engagement ring, they insisted — and she had fun catching the light in its facets. We felt as though the whole world was sparkling and that a great boulder had been lifted from our shoulders.

We telephoned the nice woman agent at Uzerche, who had been waiting all week to know our decision. We were sorry not to be buying from her because we liked her and admired her professionalism. We said her house had been one of our three top choices but that we had fallen in love with another one. She was philosophical. "I am very sorry," she said, "but I understand. We have a saying, 'the nest must be built where the nest must be built.'"

We made a detour to visit St Paradis the next morning on the way back to the ferry. We'd asked for the keys so that we could measure up but they'd been sent back to the branch office and it was closed. We measured the outside and took photographs with the measuring tapes on show so that we could work out other dimensions later.

"We've bought it!" we told the neighbours. "We'll come back in September and start to work on it."

They were pleased. We were pleased. And we could have sworn that the house was pleased too.

When we got back to England our friends were amazed that we'd done what we set out to do, and with hindsight so were we. The house fitted nearly all of our preconditions and if it didn't have a wood it certainly had a lot of trees round the boundary. It really was the elusive "fantasy home" of our dreams. We couldn't believe that we had stumbled upon it by accident or had such lucky timing. A few weeks earlier and it would have been off the market during the abortive sale, a few weeks later and it really would have been too expensive, regardless of Chris's generosity.

We'd made our successful offer and paid the deposit at 8.5FF to £1 and sterling was sinking. The week we returned to England the pound started to plummet against the franc. It didn't look much on the travel agents' boards but each centime was costing us £300. When the bank transmitted the balance of the money the rate was 8.3FF. The pound continued to drop. If we hadn't bought St Paradis exactly when we did we never could have done. It would have cost thousands more.

All the formalities went through quickly and in less than six weeks, at the end of July, the Leprechaun rang to say that St Paradis was ours. We had by this time worked out why the vendor had held out for a higher sum second time around — he needed to make up the money he had lost when he mysteriously stopped the sale to the first buyer.

The formal papers which made up the *acte de vente* were fascinating. The actual price of the house had been 220,000FF and the rest of the money had gone on *notaire*'s fees, local and government taxes, and agent's commission. We were amazed to receive some "change" from the full sum of 280,000FF we'd paid: apparently it was normal to round figures up to be on the safe side. We could see from the cadastral plan exactly which plots we had bought and their numbers on the national land register. But unlike English deeds, they also traced the title of the vendor to the property. This was the first time we made Marguerite's acquaintance formally. Deciphering the legal French to the best of our ability we learned that she had inherited the house from her father who had died in 1961. She was the widow of Henri and had died in a neighbouring *département* in 1985. Because she had no direct heir the house eventually went by a complicated route to two cousins. One, a bachelor, died in 1986, so St Paradis then became the sole property of our vendor. We wondered why he had waited so long to sell it.

We started to plan for our week's visit to the house in September. We knew that it would be uninhabitable for the first few days while we did a massive cleaning job. We would be so dirty that we'd need somewhere to wash, so hungry that we'd need some good meals and so exhausted that we'd need good beds.

I looked through the lists of *chambres d'hôtes* in the area and chose one based in a *château* a few miles away, which provided an evening meal as well as bed and breakfast. Chris and Linda were both invited but Linda decided not to come because she wanted to do some last-minute study in England before they went back to university after their year out in industry. Chris was more relaxed about it all.

We amassed trunks and cardboard boxes full of household items and tools. We bought a pressure washer to tackle the grottiest jobs and a camping gas cooker for quick meals. There was soon far too much to get into two cars. We were going separately because Jack and I were to spend several days in our twin town for the opening of their new cultural centre before going on to St Paradis. Then Linda's parents came to the rescue. They were going on holiday to the Dordogne a couple of days earlier and could make a detour to St Paradis. They were happy to take a trunk if we gave them a list of its contents to show the Customs.

It was amazing how much we didn't need to buy. As confirmed hoarders we had 25 years' worth of accumulated goodies. For our wedding presents we'd asked for the components of a Wedgwood earthenware dinner service. Ten years later we suddenly discovered that after starting with at least six of everything we were down to very odd numbers in all departments — such as eight saucers and three cups. We put the remains away in tissue paper and bought another complete service at a fraction of the price from a pottery factory seconds shop in Stoke-on-Trent. So the Wedgwood was packed up for St Paradis together with all the other kitchen items and linen we'd duplicated over the years because it was boring or unfashionable.

The proprietor of our favourite market stall was retiring and disposing of his goods at silly prices. He owned a linenware mill in Lancashire and as a hobby sold samples, overmakes and out-of-date stock at our Saturday market. In the last weeks of trading I spent £25 on about £200-worth of sheets and duvet covers for St Paradis, some of which I would unpick and make into matching curtains over the next six months. There were towels from long-gone Wimbledons and a host of other bargains.

I had a whale of a time.

Jack suddenly had an excuse to acquire all the tools he really wanted. We had always intended to do the work on the house ourselves and to make a professional job of it he needed the professional gear. It was an investment — surely?

St Paradis had started to take over our lives. It still has.

Linda's kind parents had an inauspicious start and a messy finish to their expedition. The Customs demanded to know all about my innocent school trunk in the back of their estate car. The officers made a meal of asking about the contents and threatening to make her father empty and repack the car. Her mother pointed out that if she was a dangerous terrorist and a threat to British security she would hardly be taking the trunk out of the country or travelling with it on the same ferry. They eventually boarded the ship without unpacking the car but with severely raised blood pressure. When they delivered the trunk at St Paradis, we'd asked them to put it in the kitchen and to hide the front door key under the hay in one of the mangers in a far corner of the sweet-smelling barn. Linda's mother plunged her hand into the hay — grasping the corpse of something covered with a mass of maggots! They had had a quick look round the house in torchlight without opening the shutters and, unblinkered by love, had remarked secretly that they thought we'd got "an awful lot" to do. It was only in retrospect that we agreed with them.

Our bedroom windows were covered with vines and cobwebs.

Chapter Four

Chris was the first member of the family to cross the threshold at St Paradis after we'd bought the house. Our friends in Mornant had told us it wouldn't take long to drive over to the Limousin but we got stuck in Clermont-Ferrand (the curse of the "C-F word"!) and embarrassingly lost our way in the maze of lanes only a few kilometres from the house. Chris had made incredible time from Paris in his old Cavalier in spite of being weighed down with half the luggage.

So when we pulled up outside the house in mid-afternoon it was already awake and looking to the future. The shutters and windows were open and it was drinking in the sunshine and fresh air. Chris was busy in the kitchen with an old brush he'd found, tackling the cobwebs which had multiplied during the summer. Now we looked at the building with the eyes of a fond spouse rather than a besotted fiancé. What faults would our beloved reveal which we had been too blind to see before? It was much dirtier than we had remembered. Cobwebs full of dead flies dangled from the beams and clung to the walls. Black spiders lurked in the corners. There was a container of ancient pink rat poison in every room. Inexplicably, pieces of straw littered most of the floors. Each fireplace was full of rubbish covered by washed-down mortar from the chimney above. The windows were filthy. Little piles of dusty junk lay around and there were some strange grubby objects we didn't recognise, which looked old and fragile. The *cantou* contained the twisted remains of a small and truly tasteless 1960s metal side-table. The disgusting green doors upstairs were still as repulsive. The would-be salon was as uninviting. The jungle at the back was even more impenetrable.

In short, there was absolutely nothing wrong which couldn't be sorted out with a bit of elbow-grease.

The house seemed to be mutely asking for help, like a proud pensioner who has let things go and needs a good bath and some fresh new clothes. The dignity was still there, underneath.

"I was loved once," it kept saying. "Please love me again. I

41

don't want to be like this."

The first thing we did was to symbolically remove the "For Sale" poster off the front door to the salon. We hoped it would be several Loader generations before the house was for sale again. The vine was heavy with bunches of small grapes — a poor crop because it was in such need of pruning. Insects buzzed amid the fruit and a tiny lizard shot up the granite wall.

We swept the kitchen floor, unpacked the cars and quickly filled up the kitchen and back scullery with boxes. Then we put on our boiler suits and set to work. At this point we were waiting for Electricité de France (EDF) to come and reconnect the electricity and for the water company to reconnect the water. They were both due the next day. We therefore had no light, power or means of washing things, so it was just a question of applying brawn. Chris and Jack went out to threaten the jungle with our new brush-cutter and I started by going round the whole house taking "before" photographs. I hoped the "after" ones I would take at the end of the week would be significantly different.

I set up a big black plastic bag on the kitchen floor and started to fill it with the mess from the *cantou*. I threw in a magazine wrapper, then took it out. It was addressed to Marguerite and dated 1985. Some newspapers were about to join the rest of the junk when I noticed the dates: 1965. I decided to be more discerning.

In among the papers were some other publications: prewar almanacks, catalogues and what seemed to be children's school text books. I put them safely on one side to examine later.

We wanted to be welcoming and I had deliberately left the front door open. I knew that after being empty since at least 1985 the house would hold a fascination for our neighbours and it wasn't very long before one of the women we'd met before "just happened" to be passing. I went out and invited her in. As well as being friendly, I was desperate to find out as much as I could about the house.

She chattered on at great speed and I had difficulty understanding everything. But I gathered that she remembered "Madame" living there and she needed little encouragement from me to have a good look round. She identified a dusty wooden windmill in the kitchen as being a device for winding wool: it was obvious when you thought about it. She confirmed that there was a big bread oven behind the *cantou*. After showing her the bedrooms, I dragged her up into the attic and shone the torch around. The dormer windows did not illuminate every corner. She poked around and what she found brought back long-lost memories: *this* was a basket for taking your lunch to school; *that* was for putting bread in the oven; *this* was harness for a cart-horse; *that* was a broken yoke for an ox; *this* machine was for grinding grain; *those* were iron hoops for barrels; *these* were little straw hats to go over your bottles. By the time she had finished I realised we had a veritable museum on our hands. We mustn't throw anything away.

I wasn't the only one with a visitor. I heard French voices at the back of the house and walked round to investigate. I was astounded. At least a quarter of the jungle had been cut down — not by Chris and the petrol-driven brush-cutter but by a thin elderly man with a long-handled sickle which could well have come from our museum upstairs. He was teaching Chris how to swing the fearsome implement. It was the sort of thing peasants carried in the Revolution and he used it with the ease of a lifetime's experience. Watching and giving advice was an animated little man in a cap and blue cardigan. Big smiles and gesticulation were getting over the language barrier. They were all enjoying themselves hugely. I was introduced with the minimum of ceremony. This was obviously men's work and I left them to it.

Fired by what was stored in the attic I decided to see what else I could find. We'd brought an old vacuum cleaner so there was no point in doing lots of sweeping up. I could hoover the dirty floors when the power was turned on.

I went up to the large bedroom which Jack and I had already earmarked as ours. We intended to decorate it over the next few days so that we would have somewhere clean to sleep for future visits.

There was a faded red counterpane on the floor. Protected by surgical rubber gloves and a dust mask I picked it up and shook it. It had been nibbled by mice and some droppings fell out. I stuffed it in the black bag. In one corner was something I'd originally dismissed as an ancient radio but on closer inspection turned out to be a *papier maché* box with a round glass frame on the front and a lid on top. When the light was right I could just make out a picture of a 19th century man and woman under the glass. There had once been a small drawer underneath. When I opened the lid I found little knick-knacks like buttons and decorative buckles inside, all tarnished and dirty. The drawer I found on top of the mantelpiece: it contained scraps of paper and more books. The inside was filthy and I was glad of my gloves.

I prodded the rubbish in the fireplace with my boot. Out fell what looked like a crude wooden mousetrap and a tiny stool. I sat down on the floor and started to sift through the grate. More pieces of paper, going brown with age. I unfolded them gingerly, afraid of damaging them. These were letters! The writing was faded on the outside, blacker and more distinct where the light had not reached the ink. They were over 100 years old.

When I'd been through this fireplace I went into the green bedroom and started on that one. Rolls of wallpaper had been stuffed in it. When I unrolled them they showed the true colours of the red bedroom paper, now faded to pink. It had once been a vivid scarlet patterned with a yellow design. The matching border was there too, in six rows on standard sized wallpaper. The decorator must have had to cut them up himself. There were roll-ends of other designs too but these were long-gone. No sign remained of them in the house. I found a bag of tiny envelopes in a distinctive orange colour, and a board-game in excellent condition. There were more buckles and buttons and a broken photo frame. Presumably once framed in it was a photograph, sadly damaged by the ash in the fireplace, showing a serious middle-aged woman in 19th century clothing. Best of all was a folded page from a broadsheet newspaper. As a journalist I love old newspapers anyway. But when I opened this up I was staggered to find a full colour poster showing a patriotic scene with a wounded soldier. Apart from fragility round the folds it was as fresh as when it had been printed in the late 1800s. I discovered that it illustrated a novel which was being serialised on the reverse.

There was no time to examine my treasures closely but I was entranced. We'd wanted to find out about Marguerite and the family who had owned the house but we had not expected to discover so many personal items. It was important for us to establish links with the past because we felt humble about owning the house. We suspected it had been in the hands of only one family since it was built: they had lived, laboured and loved there every day for generations. We had bought it for holidays and for our retirement — it seemed too frivolous. I thought of Marguerite with no son to pass it on to and I promised solemnly: "We will look after your house, we will cherish it and we won't make any major changes to it."

It was starting to get dark and we needed to find our *chambres d'hôte* at the *château*. Jack and Chris said goodbye to their new friends after they'd worked together to do wonders to the jungle. I learned that the tall one was Michel and the little one was Paul. They had helped tirelessly all afternoon, popping home for equipment, demonstrating what to do and dispensing valuable advice. A significant part of the brambles and undergrowth was now blazing on a bonfire in the middle of the field. We were very grateful for their interest.

We spread a rug on the bedroom floor then took off our boiler suits and boots. Chris was red with exertion and sticky with sweat. Jack had been custodian of the bonfire and had spent his time dragging debris to it. They both smelled of wood-smoke and we all needed a good wash.

The *château* was hard to find. It was so well-known locally that it had long ago dispensed with such luxuries as signposts. There was just one — kilometres away — but the name was spelled differently. We gambled on this, drove up to it, lost our nerve and drove away. Ten minutes later, after consulting several residents, we decided there couldn't be two *châteaux* in such a small area. If it was the wrong one the owners surely wouldn't chop our heads off for visiting them by mistake.

It was the right one. Madame, perhaps in her late fifties, was charming and we liked her immediately. In England she would have been a dowager in pearls and green wellies; in France she was a class act in blue denims. The *château* had been in her husband's family for a thousand years. It looked out over a lake and ponies grazed in the grounds.

Our bedroom was a high-ceilinged elegant room with tall windows. Its ensuite facilities were hidden behind a pair of doors. Opening what looked like a wardrobe, we found a washbasin, associated cupboards and an ancient gas geyser. We were reminded to extinguish the flames before we closed the doors. Jack, imbued with Health and Safety Regulations, blanched visibly.

Chris had a smaller room with a washbasin down the corridor. We shared a lavatory on the landing. Anyone wishing for a bath or shower could have one in a room with equipment straight out of a 1930s brochure. Madame hinted that as we were a little late, showers before dinner might cause something of a problem. Our fellow guests were elderly and liked to eat exactly on time. We took the hint and washed in our bedrooms.

She served the meal at a traditional long table in a newer part of the *château*, probably dating back to the 1700s. Our companions for the night were an elderly blind man, who had lost his sight in an accident, and his slightly younger wife. He had been in the Resistance and was determined to tell his tale. When the familiar words started his wife's eyes glazed over: she must have heard them thousands of times before. She cut up his food, guided his fork and let him hold forth. We were exhausted, emotionally and physically and Chris's grasp of French was less than ours, though his O Level marks were better. We tried our best to understand but can remember only that the story involved the old man being an interpreter for the Germans whilst giving information to the Resistance, travelling on trains with various forged passes and having lots of narrow escapes. It was sad that we couldn't do him justice, though we ooh'ed and aah'ed in the right places and made him feel appreciated. From the way Madame's eyes also glazed over, we suspected that she had listened to the same story, word for word, the previous night or maybe every night for the previous week. Her husband joined us for the dessert: a typical French intellectual and gentleman. He was courteous and interesting, and managed to divert the old man enough to ask us about our house. I told him about all the things I'd found and he was genuinely intrigued. I promised to bring some of them in the following evening.

But the most fascinating aspect of the conversation was when I talked about my mother at Saumur. He replied that his father had been a cavalry officer in charge of the Cadets at exactly the time my mother had been there. It seemed that the French tentacles reaching to our family through the generations were as strong as ever.

The next day we were expecting men to come and reconnect the water and electricity. We had written to EDF from England giving them a date when we were due to arrive, and through the Leprechaun we had discovered that the local mayor (*maire*) was responsible for organising someone to do the water. Leaving Chris at home to lubricate the shutter hinges with WD40, Jack and I went down to the tiny town hall (*mairie*) to introduce ourselves to the *maire* and check that he had received our letter. We'd had no acknowledgement and were worried that we might be waterless. Paul had told us that the civic leader was available to his con-stituents every Tuesday morning.

The *mairie* conformed to the usual design. It filled the centre of the village's most imposing building, flanked on either side by what had once been the girls' and boys' departments of a little pri-mary school. Rural depopulation meant they were now closed. Passing under the tricolour over the front door, we waited our turn in a large public room with metal chairs along the walls. A map of the commune was on display. This was where the *maire* would conduct local civil marriages.

When it was our turn we went into a side office and faced him over a high wooden counter. He was very helpful and welcoming. Yes, of course he remembered our letter: the man from the water company was coming that morning and might already be at the house. Jack and I had both been councillors in Cheshire. We all exchanged local government chat and compared systems of administration. Monsieur le Maire was far more powerful than either of us had been as chairman of our parish council, although he had a fraction of the number of constituents. While we were talking the postman arrived with the *mairie*'s letters. We were introduced and shook hands. A shambling bear of a man with ginger hair, he was very friendly and promised to redirect any mail for us which might arrive when we were in England. We wrote out our Cheshire address on a scrap of paper and he tucked it in his pocket.

We drove five minutes into the nearest town — with a population of all of 800 — and bought some bread, butter and paté for lunch. Going back to the house we agreed that we were beginning to feel at home.

A few minutes later the "water man" arrived in his van. We had no idea where the stop-cock and meter were. The search provided great entertainment for Paul and Michel who were already giving Chris a hand at the back. The engineer started to "dowse" for the water-main with a metal detector. He went all over the place in a delightfully random pattern before he realised he was detecting the metal toecaps in his own boots. We eventually tracked down the tap and meter under a concrete slab in the barn and were ceremonially turned on. Water started to pour on to the path by the kitchen window. I discovered that the cold tap above the kitchen sink had been left on — and that the sink drained directly from a rubber pipe through a hole in the wall on to the path and down the slope into a flowerbed. The lavatory might be connected to the septic tank but the other drainage was more basic.

There was still no sign of EDF. We didn't know what the man had to do physically to re-establish the power. The house had been empty for so long that it was highly unlikely that the electricity would still be connected. We thought it wouldn't hurt to throw the switch on the meter, though we expected nothing to happen. But it did — the lights came on! We took a note of the meter reading for future reference. Now we could plug in our old mini fridge and really stock up with food for our lunches.

We were busy in the house when there was a loud hoot followed by a banging on the front door. It was Paul, telling us that the twice-weekly baker's van had arrived further up the road. I took my purse and went outside. A mobile shop pulled up outside and the back was rolled up by a pleasant-looking woman to reveal a miniature *boulangerie*. I bought three extravagant cakes for our lunch and made friends with the shopkeeper. She gave Paul a large loaf.

We ate in style. Chris sat on a plank over a crate full of empty mineral water bottles which we'd found in the dining room. Jack and I balanced on our very own drums of cable. We didn't possess a table.

After lunch Jack and I decided to go to the *départemental* capital where we had opened our bank account so that we could collect our chequebook and make ourselves known. We also needed some food and some electrical sockets and adaptors so that we could make the most of our one power point. We left Chris behind in case EDF arrived.

When we returned in mid-afternoon Chris and the neighbours were doing a magnificent job round the back. Not only was the jungle receding but they had dragged a lot of the ivy off the wall. They had also discovered a flight of granite steps, covered with soil, moss and algae, leading to an oak back door. The frame was of granite blocks carved to take the shape of the door. It was nothing like the elegant facade at the front, more like something from the Middle Ages. We hadn't really registered before that we had a back door. It had been covered with ivy and led to an almost medieval space under the staircase. While the kitchen floor was concrete the floor here was rough-hewn rock like the cellar. The stairs stretched up across a corner of the door as though they had been built as an after-thought many years later, and we discovered two ancient fire-axes on iron brackets let into the side of the staircase. It was a spooky place.

Chris, an electronic engineer then working for a French company, and Jack, a research scientist, had few qualms about tackling the electrical system, even though it was three-phase and mostly dated back to the 1930s. I wouldn't recommend this to anyone who didn't know what they were doing. They had soon fixed up the pressure washer and Jack started to clean the steps. In no time it had scoured off years of dirt to reveal beautifully-cut granite blocks, fitted together with great skill.

In clearing the brambles as far as the back wall, Chris, Paul and Michel had also uncovered relatively new plastic pipes connecting the lavatory to the septic tank and an ugly green stain down the wall from the eaves to the ground which showed where rainwater had cascaded through a hole in the zinc guttering. It had bounced off the windowsill to our prospective bathroom and splashed back, accounting for the damp in the wall around the window. Over the years it had actually worn a triangular hole in the windowsill. Jack pressure-washed this stain away, leaving the wall a uniform grey. We were interested to contrast how much work had gone into the meticulous pointing of the almost Georgian (by British standards) front of the house, while the back had been left rough and traditional. Judging by the fact that the staircase simply didn't fit, we wondered how often the house had been extended and "modernised" during its life.

While the men cleaned the outside, I was busy inside with the brush and hoover. Just cleaning the floors and sucking up the dust and cobwebs made an enormous difference. But oh, that dust and cobwebs! The only way to deal with them was to go for total body coverage — boiler suit, boots, gloves, dust-mask and headscarf. A worker at Sellafield would have been proud of me. My glasses stopped the long-dead creepy-crawly bits falling in my eyes though they got steamed up when the dust-mask deflected all my breath up and on to the lenses. Sometimes it felt like a choice between breathing and seeing. The house wasn't as dirty as many we'd seen when we were looking at properties, but it was the dirtiest I'd ever had to deal with. The saving grace was that each sweep of the brush and each swoop of the vacuum cleaner made a tangible improvement.

Chris went into the red bedroom for something while Jack stepped by for a word with me. We heard a crash and muffled swearword. Chris came out with a newspaper parcel tied up with old-fashioned string.

"I'm sorry, I think I've broken some glass," he said. "I didn't see it and caught it with my boot."

We undid the parcel. He was right. The pane of glass had been neatly wrapped up and placed beneath a window where there was a crack. It would have fitted exactly.

"Hang on a minute," said Jack. "Look at the date of this paper!"

We examined it. The main story was about Marshal Petain in 1941.

"I've heard of people putting off DIY jobs," said Jack. "But putting them off for more than 50 years must be a record."

That night at the *château*, the old blind man started on his story again. We'd only heard it once but we recognised the opening gambit. Undeflected by anyone's efforts to change the subject, he told us everything, word-perfect. I was annoyed that I had forgotten to take my treasures from St Paradis: he might have enjoyed hearing about them.

After supper, Madame reminded us that when we had made our booking she had told that she was taking her old people's club on an outing to Vichy on Thursday. She was sorry but she would be leaving at 6am and would not have time to make a meal in the evening: this of course would be reflected in our bill at the end of the week. We were happy about this — it would give us an excuse for a little shopping.

Next morning, Wednesday, Jack wanted to relight the bonfire. He went into the salon and took a newspaper at random from a pile behind the door. He was just going to screw it up when he saw that the headlines were about Mussolini's final ultimatum to the Greeks in October 1940. We had yet another addition to our stack of treasures.

We had given up waiting for EDF. The water worker had arrived so promptly that we thought the electricity chap might have been round on the Monday morning before we arrived and had done what needed to be done without coming inside the building. We were pleased because we'd read that EDF were very strict with foreigners who mucked about with French wiring, and we couldn't hold back any longer. Jack and Chris weren't happy with the one electric socket in the house. It was beside the kitchen window and we were using it as the source for a couple of extension leads which enabled us to have power upstairs and downstairs. They thought a bit of modification would be in order and unscrewed it from the wall. They worked out some wiring diagrams on the back of an envelope and Jack left Chris to do the job, surrounded by electrical tools, cables, extension leads, sockets, plugs and bits of wire which might come in handy.

Then there was a knock at the door and we saw the EDF van through the kitchen window. Should we keep the man at bay until Chris had covered up the evidence of our nefarious activities or should we plead ignorance? We chickened out and let him in. Stepping carefully over the drums of cable and four-gang extension sockets, he headed straight for the meter. Had we illegally tampered with company property? He satisfied himself that the seals were still in place and I came up trumps with the exact meter reading from the day before, which tallied with his records. He filled in his forms, gave us the paperwork to pay by direct debit, shook hands all round, negotiated the cable assault course and went out for a chat with Paul — who had appeared as if by magic. Then he consulted his watch, decided it must be lunchtime and sped off in his little van, quite happy.

We breathed an enormous sigh of relief. What would we have done with a "Jobsworth"?

After a quick lunch we decided to treat ourselves to a trip to the nearest city. As a family we're connoisseurs of French hypermarkets and were already suffering withdrawal symptoms.

We decided to buy a plastic table and four chairs which we could put in the kitchen to start with and relegate to the garden when the kitchen was more respectable. It currently resembled a chaotic workshop rather than a room in a house.

We had misjudged things. Although it was early September and the weather was still very pleasant, the shops regarded it as the season of the *"Rentrée"* ("Back to School"). All the garden furniture had been sold and everywhere was full of books, pens, paper and school bags. It looked as if we would have to continue to eat off our knees while sitting on cable drums and the plastic crate. Then at the last moment we found a pine table and two benches for not much more than we would have paid for the plastic equivalents. We bought them and a set of wooden shelves so that I could begin to unpack all our boxes and make the place more homely. On the way home we stopped and bought some glass for a broken window pane in our bedroom, The cracked one could wait — though not another 50 years.

Our shopping had taken a long time. We stopped off at the house to unload and I picked up the books, letters and other documents I'd found on the first day. I'd been too busy to examine them very closely.

Looking at an ethics textbook in the pile, I was curious about its very thick cover, which seemed to be of a strange stiff material. I peeled it off and found that the padding underneath was made of five or six folded sheets of exercise book paper covered with neat writing in Indian ink. It was French grammar homework, and very difficult stuff, too. It was also dated: 1877! I turned to the stiff covering with mounting excitement when I noticed spidery writing on it. It was a legal document on parchment written out by a *"Notaire Royale"*, which dated it before the Revolution. The corners had been chopped off to make it fit the shape of the book. The text was very faded and the writing was of another era, very hard to decipher. Not knowing legal French, it could just as well have been written in Latin. At the end it was possible to make out the name "Xavier" — Marguerite's maiden name and the name of the family who had owned the house for generations. Under the name was what looked like the date, 1746. Inside the book, in boyish handwriting, was the message "This book belongs to André Xavier, St Paradis, 1877." It was extraordinary to think of young André finding, or being given, a family parchment which was already 130 years old to keep the dirt off his expensive textbook.

We took our little box of "finds" along to the *château* that night to show Monsieur after dinner. We diverted the old man with our discoveries and when the table was cleared he listened closely to his wife's descriptions of what we had spread out there.

The parchment was our most spectacular item, but the letters were more poignant. The oldest were between Xavier brothers in the last decades of the 19th century. They were homely but formal messages, like: "Dear Brother-in law, I have the threshing machine on Saturday and Sunday. If my nephew could come on the Sunday, I would be very pleased. I know that it is the fair that day but if he will help us during the day we can go together afterwards." "My dear brother, Can you help me to get in the hay? I have been ill. Must stop now, the postman is waiting."

The most fascinating were written by the family to Marguerite's father when he was a soldier during the First World War. The men were mobilised by the Government so quickly and with so little thought that many Limousin farms were left without strong young men and were run by the women and the old men. Marguerite, then aged about 15, wrote to her father: "I had the dressmakers here to make me a summer dress. Mummy and Uncle have harrowed the field at the Wood with the oxen twice today, and the land at the Little Wood once. After dinner they put the cultivator twice over the Little Wood and this morning they did it twice in succession at the Big Wood. We are tending the potatoes and haricot beans..."

Another relative (perhaps the "uncle" mentioned before) wrote: "It is January 1, 1915 and a new year is before us. Here are my wishes: a happy new year; good health; a complete crushing of the Boches; total victory for the Allies; general peace, the return of Alsace and Lorraine, complete liberation — and the return of all our friends who are so sorely missed..." He spoke of what appeared to be two women who were inconsolable after the departure of Marguerite's father and continued for a while apparently quoting their comments in *patois*. He told a funny story about a neighbour trying to duck conscription and described what work was being done on the farm.

There were also some letters which Marguerite had written in pencil, on the backs of other letters, as if she had been practising what to say. These were ordering items from the many agricultural and pharmaceutical catalogues which I had also found. The family had obviously been interested in all the latest farming methods and products. They had also been avid consumers of patent medicines for every ailment possible. Indeed in those days one product would claim to heal at least a dozen apparently unrelated conditions.

Monsieur, who lived amid a thousand years of his own family history, was fascinated by it all and knowledgeable too. He could make out what the letters said, although they were faint, but the parchment was too damaged to translate in detail. He identified the orange envelopes as being for an election and we found among the scraps of paper an election address by a member of the family from the beginning of the 1900s in which he promised to do all the things that politicians have promised since the dawn of time. One of the buttons in the drawer had come from a gendarme's uniform, Monsieur thought.

We had the impression that the house wanted to tell us about itself. It wasn't an inanimate construction of stone and timber. It was somewhere that had been a home to people who were well-educated, leaders of the community and reasonably well off, with a thriving farm. From the depths of the country they had kept up to date with the latest trends and fashions. They had been torn apart by the First World War and stoically carried on. The last of their line had met an untimely death in the Second World War and now they were fighting against oblivion — or someone was fighting on their behalf.

We had broken the back of the jungle outside.

Chapter Five

Next morning no breakfast was served at the *château*, so we got up early and bought fresh bread and croissants in the town on the way to the house. After a quick meal we all went outside to explore the newly revealed landscape at the back. For not only did we have a back door and a set of steps to it, we had found outbuildings which we never knew existed. They had been covered up completely by the jungle and were not even visible on the photographs we had taken when we visited the house to measure up in June. At right angles to the house there was a stone stable and hen-house with a wood store above, and we discovered a locked door leading to the bread oven building which was alongside the kitchen. I was the first to investigate the henhouse and was astounded to find a plastic egg lying on a hen-shaped indentation in the hay-lined laying boxes.

I had by now cleaned all the floors, walls and ceilings in the house and it was time to start on more cosmetic things. We had discovered active woodworm in the floor of the green bedroom and on our journey to the city the day before we'd bought a litre of woodworm zapper as an experiment. I found it was impossible just to apply it to the holes because it stained the wood dark brown, so I started to paint it systematically on the floorboards. It looked really attractive — almost like varnish. I'd completed only six boards when the fluid ran out. Ironically the floor in this room was much newer than the others and poorer quality wood. The rest of the house had thick uneven oak floorboards — where if you looked closely at a plank you could see each laborious stroke of the saw which had cut it — but these were narrower and neatly planed. Whether the floor had been replaced for aesthetic or structural reasons we did not know. Perhaps the work had been done at the same time the beams had been boxed in?

Chris, Michel and Paul had broken the back of the jungle outside and Chris was aching all over with the use of unaccustomed muscles. Michel might have spent a lifetime with the slasher but it was a new experience for our son. He decided to indulge in some light relief by painting the modern concrete block wall in the lavatory and back kitchen with white matt paint we'd brought from England. I had also carefully chosen some Dulux peach coloured emulsion to go with my colour scheme for our bedroom. We said he could have a go with that, if he liked.

Jack discovered to his embarrassment that the pane of glass we'd bought for our bedroom window was fractionally too small. He'd had an uncharacteristic mental aberration when he'd measured it up.

We decided we'd have to go back to the *départemental* capital to get some more supplies. On the way back we stopped off at the St Paradis village cemetery to see if we could find any trace of Marguerite and her family. Michel had said she was buried there, in spite of having died elsewhere.

Chris and Jack had spent most of their time working congenially with Paul and Michel, who would "just happen" to pass whenever they started a new project and would join in with gusto. But I had passed many hours on my own in the house and I had found that my mind turned constantly to Marguerite, especially after our examination of the letters and documents. She had became more and more real to me and I very much wanted to know what she had looked like. Then it had suddenly occurred to me that there might be a picture on her grave, in keeping with the local custom.

The grave was not hard to find. It was one of the biggest and most imposing in the whole cemetery and it looked down directly on the roof of our house. It was dedicated to the Xavier family and had a glass canopy over three sides to protect it from the weather. There were three photographs. One of a rather plain young woman in a traditional white head-dress we took to be Marguerite in her youth. It was attached to the main crucifix headstone. On top of the stone vault were two marble memorials. A black one, like an open book, recorded the death of Marguerite's "dear husband" who had died at the age of 75 in 1968. He must have been about seven years her senior. The other was a more elaborate white tablet on a stand. Two crossed tricolours were set under a photograph of their "dear son", a bright young man with a remarkable resemblance to Chris. Gold lettering recorded that he was born in 1921 and arrested at Clermont-Ferrand University in November 1943 when he was a pharmacy student. He was described as a *résistant* and political deportee who had died for France. He had disappeared at Thérézin in Czechoslovakia on May 6, 1945. *"Regrets"* it said at the bottom in capital letters. "Greatly missed..."

It was very moving. I vowed I would find out all I could about this Thérézin place and what had happened to him. We felt strangely reassured that Marguerite could "see" the house so well from her grave and sorry that only her photograph was there. She had no written memorial.

When we returned we found that Chris had finished downstairs and had painted one 18ft x 8ft wall in the bedroom with a roller. The plaster on the wall was ancient and thirsty. He had used almost an entire five-litre can of peach paint costing £19.99. By my calculations that should have done the entire room! We abandoned the roller and I took over with a three-inch paintbrush, using a second can which I had originally bought to provide a finishing coat. But first I put ten litres of woodworm killer on the green bedroom floor. It went on easily and made an enormous difference. Suddenly one could begin to see the room as an elegant *boudoir*.

Chris shouted. He had been cleaning out under the staircase and had found a mummified rat in a nest of chewed-up wallpaper. Only the skin and teeth remained: the body was absolutely flat. It was big and we were glad it was dead. Perhaps all the rat poison we had found when we took over the house had been to some effect.

At 9pm we stopped and had our first evening meal in the house: my holiday cholesterol-rich standby of ham, eggs, baked beans and tinned new potatoes, finished off with cakes from the town *boulangerie*. We washed it all down with a bottle of champagne, given to us in Mornant as a present from the Twinning Committee. We video-ed ourselves popping the cork and drinking a toast to St Paradis. Afterwards we kept the bottle as a souvenir and put an artificial flower arrangement in it. Apart from the menu, it was a memorable landmark in our occupation of the house. The next was to be Saturday night — we had promised ourselves that we would sleep at St Paradis during this stay, if only for one night, however primitive the accommodation might be. Each day's work showed a significant improvement and the house was gradually transforming itself back into a dwelling-place.

Friday was a long slog. Chris had once been fit. He and Alex had spent years competing in canoe slalom competitions and then Chris had taken a weekend and holiday job as a fitter in a local boatyard. He had been accustomed to manual labour. But two years at University and a third working at Michelin had left him soft, physically. Now he was working ten hours a day as a labourer and house renovator and it was hurting. I sympathised. Painting three walls of an 18ft square bedroom with a three-inch brush to economise on paint took seven hours. I ran out of peach paint with about six square feet to go. I also ran out of energy. But our bedroom looked wonderful. It actually looked like a bedroom. I hoped Marguerite approved.

Meanwhile Jack and Chris had been performing miracles on the exterior of the house. They knew they needed a big ladder and had looked it up in the dictionary so they knew what to ask for. It was an *échelle*. They told Paul, whose step-daughter Anne-Marie lent them an enormous ladder which she in turn had borrowed from a neighbour at the bottom of the road. This reached up ten metres and allowed Jack to repair the damaged zinc guttering at the back by superglueing in a piece of zinc he'd found in the undergrowth. Then he spotted a more minor hole, and Paul and Michel nodded in approbation as he mended it with a piece of plastic Orangina bottle and silicone bath sealant. Our DIY style obviously accorded with theirs. While he was up the ladder he pulled off the remaining pieces of stubborn ivy and for the first time we were able to see the back of the house free of any vegetation. It was incredible to think that only days before it had all been covered up.

The ladder was extremely heavy and hard to handle. It was impossible for one person to manoeuvre. The men carried it round to the front where they set about pruning the all-enveloping vine. Paul and Michel advised on the technique. It was important, they stressed, to cut it right back to the main stems even if this meant there was no crop next year. It would recover eventually. The main snag was the fury of a tenacious hornet who objected to his juicy grape lunch being demolished.

As the vine was cut away the character of the house became more apparent and we could admire the beautiful craftsmanship of the stonemasons who had built it. Undamaged by pollution, the granite was clean and the pointing was still attractively picked out with reddish lines. In the stone lintel above the front door we found a date: 1806. We did not know if this referred just to the front or to the whole house — the back part seemed almost timeless and we would have expected it to be older. Yet even if the entire place had been built in 1806, it was still pretty remarkable. England and France had been at war then. Napoleon had been Emperor for two years and Nelson had died at the Battle of Trafalgar the year before. How many generations of Xaviers had lived there since then?

Before we returned to the *château* for our last night, I put on my gloves and went into the salon. I had been avoiding this room as beyond redemption but I thought I would have a little poke about while I recovered from the painting. By the back wall I found a disintegrating crate full of filthy bottles. I took one out and wiped it down my boiler suit. It had once held Vichy water. As the dust slipped off I could see that the label was almost in mint condition. Dates mentioned on it were about the turn of the century. While a lot of other bottles had damaged labels, many were nearly as good as new. I picked the best to give to Monsieur and Madame as a little present. He had said we mustn't throw anything away and she had taken her old people's club on an outing to Vichy. We had liked the pair very much — it would be a suitable memento of us and they could sling it in a bottle bank if they didn't want it.

At supper that night we discovered that the old couple had moved on and our fellow guests were a Belgian couple who had bought an old cottage in the South of France. They used the *château* as a half-way house on their journeys to and from it. We had a few minutes before the meal was served and we all sat in a lounge where there was a very old hand-drawn map of the area on the wall and fascinating books of old photographs on the coffee table. We picked out St Paradis on the map and looked up its population in a list written at the bottom. It had once been much more prosperous. The pictures in the books gave us a fascinating insight into how things might have been.

During supper the Belgians said they had kept their cottage in its original state. They used oil lamps and candles for light, the well for water and a privy in the garden. They sank into a timewarp and forgot about the modern world while they were there. We thought, privately, that this was going a bit too far. Our one power point had enabled us to do a great many jobs more quickly and efficiently than we could otherwise and the lights allowed us to work when it was dark. Our well water, we suspected, might be polluted by Paul's drains — which seemed as primitive as our own. We could usually tell what he'd had for lunch by inspecting the rivulets of washing-up water running down the shallow ditch beside the lane.

Next morning we gave Monsieur and Madame their 90-year-old Vichy water bottle and said emotional goodbyes. We invited them to a housewarming party when St Paradis was habitable, and hoped it wouldn't be too long. They embraced us and said we belonged to the Limousin now.

Jack and Chris did as many jobs as they could while they still had the long ladder and I painted the finishing touches in the bedroom, which we were going to use that night. I painted the deep insides of the window frames white, in contrast to the pink walls, and picked out the plaster edge of the fireplace too. The room looked clean, rustic and inviting. I had long ago made some curtains to match the turquoise and peach duvet cover I intended to use when we installed a bed and we had spent a fortune on French wooden curtain rails. I hoped Jack would have time to put them up before we slept in there.

Eventually it was time to return the ladder and I was called to come along in case an interpreter was needed. I didn't know why they asked me. I found the delightful Paul and Michel almost incomprehensible. As far as I could tell they were speaking the French equivalent of Glaswegian. They didn't teach you *patois* at grammar school.

Jack and Chris carried the ladder between them and I had charge of the bottle of wine which we'd bought as a "thank you". We met the owner outside his house, a former inn. It was still possible to read *"Auberge Dubois"* in faded letters across the front of the building — a reminder of the days when St Paradis could support such a business. He took the wine in one hand and swung the ladder over his shoulder with the other. Jack and Chris were flabbergasted. The neighbour didn't look twice as strong as they were.

We were invited in and met his mother again. She was one of the women who had welcomed us initially and we had chatted several times since then. She was not a native of the area and her accent was easy to understand. I had never quite gathered her name, which seemed to have a lot of x's in it. From that day onwards, talking among ourselves, she became *"Madame Echelle."*

We sat round her kitchen table and drank Ricard. It was a revelation. Up until now we had always apologised to neighbours who came into our dark kitchen. We were pretty sure it hadn't been decorated since before the war and were conscious of the bare concrete floor. All our French friends in other parts of the country had expensively tiled floors and posh units. Madame Echelle's kitchen was exactly the same as ours, down to the pattern on the concrete. The only difference was the freezer which was topped by a television. She laughed at a repeated scrabbling noise coming from a shoe box on the mantelpiece over the *cantou* and showed us its contents — three baby hares in a bed of hay. "My sons found them," she said. "The babies have lost their mother so I will look after them." She had a piece of land opposite the house where she raised geese, goats, hens and ducks, and had a vegetable garden. There were some rabbit hutches, too. We imagined it wouldn't be long before the Echelle family had jugged hare for lunch.

Her son showed us his hunting horn which was hanging on

the wall. He said it was the village shoot the next morning so we were not to be alarmed if we heard guns going off. Every hunter with a gun and a dog would be there. We resolved to keep well out of the way.

That afternoon Paul and Michel congratulated Chris and Jack on their magnificent efforts outside. Paul had seen the house when it was a dusty mess, so I invited him in to view the transformation. He was reluctant: I was after all only a woman who had been pottering about amusing herself while the men did the real work. He came upstairs out of politeness. But when he saw the bedroom his eyes lit up.

"Oh la la!" he exclaimed. *"C'est incroyable!"*

He spat on his hand, clasped my shoulder and said something complimentary. I didn't catch it but if he had been a football manager it would have been "The girl done good!" From that moment on we were bosom pals.

Later I went round taking my "after" photographs. It was very pleasing to see that we had achieved so much in such a short time. I took a picture of the back of the house from the little lane which ran down the side. When I had finished I found a young woman on the path. I excused my boiler suit and we got chatting. She asked when we were coming back and I said we hoped to make it in the New Year — would it be very cold?

"It can go down to minus six degrees in the winter," she said. "But you have a fireplace, don't you? If you need any logs, just come and ask. After all, you're one of us — you're not strangers!"

I was so moved I could have kissed her. We had never even met before. I hugged the words to my heart: *"Vous n'êtes pas étrangers!"* We belonged! We were accepted!

After supper we got our bedroom ready. We had brought three inflatable mattresses and some sleeping bags. There were extra blankets in the trunks. The first problem was that it took about half an hour to blow up each mattress with a primitive foot-pump and the second was that we had lost the stopper to one of the mattresses. I volunteered to sleep on the floorboards: the other two were driving and needed a good night's sleep.

We had intended to go to bed early but somehow we couldn't

stop working. I decided to clear up the salon, however repulsive I found it. Jack and Chris were working out the back. We decided the easiest thing was for me to open the salon windows and throw things out. There was a large amount of oak leaning against the wall near the fireplace and many wooden items which were riddled with woodworm. The sooner we got them out of the room the better or the woodworm would infect the good oak and spread back into the bedroom floor above.

I picked up each plank with difficulty and threw it out, Many still bore bark along the edges and once again the saw-marks were clear. The planks formed a sort of teepee against the wall. A piece of paper slipped out. I looked at it closely. It was a cardboard sales tag from a piece of working clothing with "1923" written on it. At the bottom of the pile I found my own mummified rat. I picked it up by the tail and dropped it on the bonfire. Outside, Jack and Chris were categorising the wood. Pieces eaten beyond redemption by woodworm went for firewood, good pieces were sorted by size and put in the stable or barn for later use. Junk like chairs with two legs, rusty oilcans and old cardboard boxes ended up on the bonfire.

Later, when we knew the price of seasoned oak, we realised that I had been throwing hundreds of pounds' worth of wood around with gay abandon.

The floor was covered with a soft dust which had been extruded over the years from the woodworm crevices in the spongy planks. Often a stiff brush stripped away layers of the wood, revealing the tunnels made inside by the insects. My dust-mask was very necessary.

I swept up as best I could and was satisfied. The salon was still a horrible room but at least it was emptier and cleaner.

We went to bed at one o'clock in the morning. While I struggled to get comfortable on the floorboards, Jack and Chris rolled around on their inflatables, equally sleepless. The smell of paint was very strong. With the shutters closed it was pitch black but the room was welcoming.

We woke in the morning to the sound of dogs howling. Jack

opened the shutters quickly. It was like the "midnight barking" in *The Hundred and One Dalmatians*: we could imagine the message being passed round the village. "We're going hunting today, get ready!"

Then someone over towards the Echelles' house blew a hunting horn and at least half a dozen dogs tumbled over themselves down the road for their big day out, baying with delight. It was like something out of a cartoon and is stamped indelibly on our memories.

Jack is the most wonderfully patient person at all times except when he is packing a car. I knew from experience that it was a good idea to be out of the way. I had sudden urge to go up into the attic to see if I could find any more treasures. It felt as if Marguerite was encouraging me and although I felt guilty about diverting myself from the final clean-up, I answered the call. I had already looked round cursorily but this time I started to move things. I stooped under the cart-horse tack hanging from one of the eaves and looked at a large stack of bottles in detail, dusting each one off. There weren't many wine bottles but there were scores of medicine bottles and medicine containers. Like the Vichy water bottles, some of the medicine bottles were in superb condition with bright coloured labels and lurid descriptions of diseases. Some even had stains in the bottoms where the contents had dried up perhaps a hundred years earlier. In a different, dark part of the attic, something brushed my hair. My flesh crept, assuming it was a really repulsive cobweb. Then I discovered that I had walked into the remains of a black straw hat, hanging from a beam. It was like the ones in the old photographs at the *château*, worn by the women on special occasions. In another dark corner I found a pair of grey leather boots. They were handmade and the stitching on the soles was clearly visible. While the hat was battered, the boots were in very good condition. I could imagine feet and legs in them. I carried some of the medicine bottles, the hat and the ghostly boots downstairs and put them in a cardboard box, meaning to take them home to England with some of the other finds. Then I had an overwhelming feeling that the hat and boots must stay in the house and that it would be a gross betrayal to remove them. I left them on the floor in the bedroom. I felt about the boots as I did about the salon — decidedly ambivalent.

I returned to my last-minute cleaning and went round the house with the log-book we had been keeping, which was full of lists, measurements and diagrams. I wrote down all the jobs we had done in five and a bit days. The list filled four sides of A4 ruled paper.

Meanwhile Jack and Chris were repairing the back door. From the inside daylight was visible through the cracks between the oak planks and without its armour of ivy the door was only held closed by an ancient hook made by the local blacksmith. You could see where it had been hammered on the anvil. The men reinforced the door with one of the oak planks we had taken from the salon then fitted a bolt which shot into a hole they drilled into the granite door-frame. Paul was relieved — he had a thing about burglars and some of our tools were worth stealing.

We heard banging noises all morning from every side of the village and wondered what the hunters could be shooting. We had heard in the past from French friends that almost anything that moved was fair game and that some hunters had to put bells on their dogs' collars so they didn't shoot them by accident.

At lunchtime Madame Echelle's son came to the front door with a fresh carp. He wanted to give it to us as a present, but Jack had to explain sadly that we were leaving shortly and that it would go off before we could get it back to England.

"Never mind," said the ladder owner. "We'll put it in the freezer and you can have it next time!"

Once again, we were overwhelmed by our neighbours' simple kindness. And we couldn't help wondering if they'd shot the carp by mistake.

After the cars were packed and a few minutes before we were due to set off, Paul came over carrying a bottle of wine. He put it down on the kitchen table and took four glasses out of various trouser and cardigan pockets. We tried to combine grateful acceptance of a gesture of friendship with fears of being breathalysed or going to sleep at the wheel. We had at least six hours of driving ahead. Paul eventually understood that we really couldn't have second helpings. He put the cork back in the bottle and gave it to us.

"Finish it on the boat," he said.

Cautiously we asked if he would mind keeping a key of the house to let in the occasional meter-reader.

"Of course," he said. "And I will come in every day to make sure everything is all right."

We exchanged full names and addresses so that we could get in touch if there was an emergency. We saw his surname was "Dufour."

We gave him a bottle of whisky and a little present for his wife, whom only Chris had met. We thanked him for everything — his advice, his fatherly interest and his welcome. We embraced, shook hands and said our farewells.

We finished his wine on the ferry and we've kept the bottle. It stands in my office at home — full of silk flowers — and we think of Paul whenever we look at it. We all have been devoted to each other ever since.

Chapter Six

B ack home in Cheshire we started to prepare for our New Year
visit. The main priority was to get as much furniture over
there as we could, so that we could actually live in the house
while we did all the other renovation work. We needed at least a
bed, a cooker and a fridge-freezer in order to sleep and eat and we
wanted some sources of extra warmth too. We'd both been children in the 1940s and '50s, with no such luxury as central heating,
and were under no illusions just how uncomfortable St Paradis
might be when it was minus six degrees Centigrade outside.

I was determined to find out as much as I could about what
might have happened to Alain and discovered to my surprise that
I was beginning to carry on a sort of dialogue with Marguerite in
my head. She seemed to be helping me to find the evidence. I
went to the library and scoured its Second World War section for
books about the French Resistance. I picked out a number but
none of them mentioned Clermont-Ferrand or Thérézin. I was
beginning to despair but Marguerite insisted that I should carry
on. Then I had a brainwave. Alain had been captured and deported to Czechoslovakia so Thérézin must have been some sort of
camp. The name might also have been spelled differently in Czech
or German. The search must be widened. I started to look for
books about the Holocaust and the last one in the whole Second
World War section was about survivors' tales. Without much con-
viction I consulted the index. There was no mention of Thérézin
but with a shiver down my spine I found "Theresienstadt (concentration camp)". I consulted a map in the appendix.
Theresienstadt was on the River Elbe in the Sudetanland, between
Dresden and Prague. The coincidence was too great.

For the next six weeks I read everything I could trace about
concentration camps which might contain some tiny reference to
Theresienstadt. I had thought I was well-informed but what I
learned distressed me deeply and haunted me. In the past when I
had read about the appalling atrocities perpetrated in the camps
it had been Man's inhumanity to Man which had been the over-
riding feature. Now I read about each stomach-churning outrage

The attic was a museum of French country life.

and wondered if it had happened to Alain, a young man who should have inherited my house, who was the same age as my own children when he died. I did not know how Marguerite could have lived with this sickening knowledge and felt closer to her all the time.

One illustrated book I found on the Resistance mentioned the Limousin in passing but there was nothing which might indicate why a student had been arrested at Clermont-Ferrand in the Auvergne — though it did mention a member of the Resistance who had been interrogated at the military prison there. The book contained some fascinating photographs but also some ghastly ones of torture instruments and people under interrogation being tortured.

I pieced together a sketchy scenario. The more I read about Theresienstadt, the more I was convinced that Alain could not have been there for more than a few hours or days. The town of Theresienstadt had been cleared in 1941 and turned into a ghetto for 250,000 Jews, 80,000 of whom were eventually deported to Auschwitz, Treblinka and Majdanek. Many others died of hunger. For propaganda reasons, the Nazis permitted a flourishing cultural life there. Its infamous Small Fortress, originally one of the most notorious political prisons of the Habsburg Empire, eventually assumed the character of a concentration camp.

The Xaviers were not Jewish. But in the dying weeks of the war in Europe the Germans were trying to counteract the outrage which the liberation of Belsen had created. As further concentration camps and slave-labour factories or mines were about to be over-run by the Allies the SS drove the surviving inmates by road — or put them in trains — and sent them to the few remaining camps still under German rule. Theresienstadt was one of these. In April 1945 an epidemic of both enteric and spotted fever broke out and spread quickly owing to the appalling conditions. A senior Red Cross official arrived there to make an inspection on May 2, 1945 and took over as effective administrator three days later when the SS guards made their escape. Alain "went missing" (the tombstone memorial said "*disparu*") the next day, along with many others who were ravaged by disease and malnutrition, two days before VE Day when the camp was liberated by the advancing Russians. I guessed he must have been a slave labourer who had been sent there on a death march and in a fatally weakened state had starved to death or succumbed to typhus or one of the other epidemics which was raging through the camp. That he had died so close to being liberated was obscene. His parents must have been full of hope right up to the last moment. I tried not to think of Alex and Chris facing the same fate. How would they have endured arrest, interrogation, torture, imprisonment, starvation, beatings, enslavement and an agonising march to final oblivion?

I came across only two photographs of Theresienstadt. One showed the face of a Jewish child arriving in a cattle truck, the other, taken after the liberation, showed a large empty courtyard with flat-roofed buildings on either side, a set of steps and a wall where prisoners were executed. Using one book's bibliography to find another, and so on in a long chain, I had borrowed what obscure publications I could track down through inter-library loan and from the British Library. There was naturally a great deal about the Jews at Theresienstadt but almost nothing about French Resistance deportees. I ended up knowing a lot about somewhere Alain might only have been fleetingly. But not being aware of his route to Theresienstadt I was frustrated. More research was needed in France if I ever got the opportunity. I was used to combing English books for gems of information — it would be hundreds of times more difficult with French ones.

We decided to hire a van to go to St Paradis after Christmas, when the fares and hire charges were low. However it proved more difficult to get a vehicle than we had imagined. In the run-up to Christmas English people were hiring vans, filling them to capacity with beer and wine and coming home to sell it all on the black market. The Customs had started to impound these vehicles and hire companies were getting wary. We managed to convince a local firm that we were going to fill our van with old furniture for the outward journey and wouldn't have any money left to import more than a few bottles of wine on the way home.

We bought a new pine-framed double bed, a second-hand IKEA leather sofa and a second-hand fridge-freezer. The sofa was a bargain but we discovered that the freezer would not go down to the right temperature. The seller was obstinate and didn't reply to our threatening letters. We decided to cut our losses and buy a new one in France. I re-covered an old chair that Jack's mother gave us and covered a footstool to match that we bought from a second-hand furniture warehouse. An unbelievable bargain tucked away there was a new French pressure cooker for £15 which we snapped up immediately. In a shop it would have cost at least £50. Through the local newspaper we got two portable gas heaters with bottles, to augment the log fire. We also had a lot of other furniture that we had replaced in the past and kept in case the boys needed it to furnish flats or houses. We gathered that they were both secretly relieved to be sidestepping our cast-offs.

Eventually we gathered together enough stuff to make St Paradis nicely habitable. I planned to strip the wallpaper in the red bedroom, paint it and turn it into a study. We couldn't use it as a bedroom because it connected directly with the green bedroom and whoever used it would have no privacy. With an old oak office desk, an elderly computer (for keeping records and drawing plans), a large table lamp, a pair of curtains I'd made from expensive patterned bed-sheets and the sofa, it should be a cosy den — especially with a gas fire to keep it warm.

Everything was going swimmingly. I had chosen the week after Christmas for our excursion because I felt I could leave my newspaper editor's job with a clear conscience. The first issue of the New Year was the smallest and most of it was written in advance: I could leave a skeleton staff to deal with that. But first I had to get the last issue of the year out of the way. As usual I went to the Production Department in the evening and sorted out all the last-minute problems. I drove home much earlier than the normal midnight and we took the dogs out for their nightly walk. I say "dogs" because we owned five: three bitches rescued at various times and the two puppies of one of the bitches whose boyfriend had jumped over the wall one memorable afternoon. Jack had the three big ones and I had the "babies" who were always a boisterous handful. They were all on extending leads. Halfway through the walk one of the pups decided to dance around her brother and plait the leads together. I jerked the lead hard to bring her up short and felt something snap in my right wrist. It started to hurt and I just couldn't use it. I hoped that if I ignored it, the pain would go away. It didn't.

Next morning my wrist and hand were still completely useless and I couldn't drive into work to tie up all the loose ends before we left that afternoon. I couldn't help Jack to load the van. I couldn't even take the pups to the kennels. Alex stepped into the breech magnificently, driving us to the kennels and packing the van with his father. We were glad we had rejected the fridge-freezer: it was so large that we could not have got it in.

The van was a brand-new Leyland-DAF with a few hundred miles on the clock. The radio didn't work and the gearbox was so laid back that Jack had no idea what gear he was in most of the time. Otherwise it was fine. Except that it was cold. I daren't go to the doctor in case it held us up, so I had bought some elasticated strapping from the chemist for my wrist. It was a size too small and was actually acting like a tourniquet. I had to remember to take it off occasionally before I got gangrene. Every time Jack braked it felt as though all the cold air from the back of the van whooshed forwards and enveloped me. He had a wardrobe behind him and escaped this effect entirely. I wound a scarf round my neck, jammed a woolly hat over my eyes and pulled my quilted mountaineering anorak round me. It was going to be a fun journey.

We arrived at Portsmouth in a severe gale and horizontal hailstones to discover that our P&O ferry was running an hour and a half late. Normally the ships take it easy at night so if they leave late they have the leeway to make up the time. But on this trip the weather was so rough en route that we were still an hour late arriving at Le Havre the next morning.

We started by travelling on the autoroutes but the increased toll did not compensate for the fact that we could only drive the van relatively slowly. We suspected that it was grossly overloaded, though would not have admitted to this. We decided to branch off on to the main roads, where the speed limit was still well above the maximum we could get out of the van. I was still suffering from the freezing draught and my wrist was no better. I was distraught. There was so much to do, so little time to do it and I was going to be completely useless. I couldn't hold a pen to fill in the log book, let alone paint a bedroom. I certainly couldn't help Jack to take all the heavy things out of the van. It was all going wrong.

We arrived at St Paradis at 6.30pm, ten and a half hours after we'd left Le Havre. When we opened the kitchen door we found Paul had lit a fire in the *cantou*. This transformed a tired, worried arrival into a homecoming. Before we turned the lights on the kitchen was bathed in a warm, dancing orange light. The chill had been taken off the room. We'd exchanged letters and Christmas cards with Paul and this kind gesture just cemented the relationship.

In the centre of the pine table was an envelope containing a New Year card from Jack's half-sister and her husband. We put it on the mantelpiece.

Jack backed the van up to the front door and we contemplated how on earth we were going to get the furniture out. I carried some light items with my left hand but I had no strength at all in the right.

Then Paul arrived, diffident, not wanting to be a nuisance, delighted that we were so pleased with his fire. We embraced him warmly. I showed him my wrist and explained what had happened. He asked if we wanted help unloading the van. We prevaricated. We would remove the things that weren't heavy and then perhaps tomorrow... He insisted. He is about 5ft 2ins.

The sofa was easy but wouldn't go up the stairs. The wardrobe was easy and was put in the bedroom, along with the chest of drawers, mattress and skeleton of the bed. The oak desk was incredibly heavy and wouldn't go up the stairs. Paul stood holding up his end while I decided that it was not worth them risking a hernia trying to get it round the bend in the staircase. We needed to dismantle it. The other big things went where they were supposed to and the rest was stacked in boxes in the salon.

Paul excused himself and we thanked him profusely. Five minutes later he was back. "If you haven't eaten, my wife says would you like to have some supper with us?" he asked. "It's nothing much, but you are very welcome." It was about eight o'clock. We accepted gratefully.

Though Chris had been to Paul's house on an errand, Jack and I had never had reason to go. We followed Paul across the road, across his open drain and up a steep little path which led to the main door. The house was probably even older than ours. In the kitchen a tall woman of about 70 was seated at the table, which was spread with a simple meal. She had white hair and a calm, handsome face. "This is Elisabeth," said Paul. We shook hands and sat down.

While Paul busied himself with fetching wine bottles and glasses, we told Elisabeth how kind he had been and how many heavy and awkward things he had carried upstairs without a second thought.

She smiled fondly at him. "And he is 80 years old next birthday," she said.

We were so ashamed. I had complained about my wrist whilst watching an octogenarian carrying a solid wood wardrobe and Victorian chest of drawers! I had chatted to him while he held up the end of a desk I couldn't even shift myself.

"It was nothing! My doctor says I have the heart of an ox," said Paul. We believed him.

Elisabeth thanked us for our correspondence, which she said had given them great pleasure. In it I had called Paul our "French father".

"So you, Madame Dufour, must be our French mother!" I joked.

"Oh no," she replied. "Not Madame Dufour: we are not married. And I am not French, I am Dutch."

She explained that they had two homes: her rented house at St Paradis and Paul's former bistro in a neighbouring village. They usually spent the summer at St Paradis because it was quieter and the winter at the bistro, which had central heating. This year they had decided to stay at St Paradis because the weather had been mild and, she hinted, Paul had enjoyed himself so much looking after our house. He really had been in every day to open the shutters and keep it aired.

It soon became apparent that one reason we had found Paul hard to understand was that he was deaf. He misheard what we said in our funny accents and then went off on the wrong track, so keen to communicate that he was almost buzzing and humming with pent-up words. Since we often couldn't catch the replies, we all found ourselves haring away in completely inappropriate directions on different subjects. Elisabeth kept shepherding us back on the straight and narrow, interpreting all round.

She spoke French with a Dutch Limousin accent and because she wasn't a native speaker she played as fast and loose with the grammar as we did. Comprehension was almost total! If we were really stuck she had reserves of English to call upon.

Paul, sitting at the table in his cap and cardigan, was a wonderful host true to his bistro background. With our bread and *paté* we had white wine, red wine, Ricard, brandy and *eau de vie*. Relaxed, we chatted for hours and they invited us round to see in the New Year with them the following evening. It was heartwarming to be accepted so completely. Elisabeth said that Paul missed the company of his old bistro customers and confided that before his retirement he had kept his wine prices ridiculously low to make sure his friends kept coming in for a chat.

At half-past midnight we said we really had to go. We had to make up our bed from scratch before we could sleep on it. The cold air outside accentuated the effects of the alcohol and by the time we had unpacked the bed from its cardboard boxes and attacked it with Allen keys we realised we were rather the worse for wear. Jack said he didn't mind doing up the screws if only the wood would stay still. We finally got to bed, with two hot-water bottles, at 1am and in pitch black with the shutters closed slept until 9.30am.

I hated the concrete floor in the kitchen and the first thing I did after breakfast was to cover it — one-handed — with some brown industrial carpet tiles we had acquired. Since we couldn't get the desk and the sofa upstairs we installed them in the kitchen, the sofa in front of the *cantou* and the desk where we'd abandoned it, near the bottom of the stairs. My re-covered chair and footstool went beside the sofa and a hi-fi unit that Alex had lent us stood on a tea trolley by the door to the scullery. The pine table and benches were put in the centre of the room near one of the gas fires. It was all in danger of being quite civilised.

There was a knock at the door. It was Paul and his son-in-law, who knew of a place where we might be able to get a second-hand cooker and fridge. I had said in one of my letters that I had an eye for a bargain and they obviously did, too. They couldn't bear for us to pay full price for something unnecessarily.

Sadly the second-hand dealer wasn't in when we arrived. We waited in the cold for some time and when he turned up he said he wasn't open anyway. Paul's son-in-law persuaded him to let us in — after all, we had just travelled about 20 kilometres to get there. His electrical goods were rusty and grossly over-priced but he had a barn full of reclaimed wood. We made our excuses and said we would remember him when we needed some wood. It was New Year's Eve and we felt very guilty that we had wasted a good two hours of the son-in-law's time on a busy day.

After lunch we took the van to the nearest city, where we had bought the table and benches. In a big electrical and furniture superstore we chose a relatively cheap Eastern European cooker to run on bottled gas and a big fridge-freezer. When we came to collect the cooker the warehousemen found it was damaged. We said we'd have the one on display. That was damaged too, in a different place. They asked us to come back the following week but we said we had to have a cooker that day or we couldn't eat, so they "married" the two to give us one unblemished piece of equipment. Unfortunately they forgot to transfer the instructions, so there are still functions of it which are a mystery to us. On the way back we stopped at the ironmongers in the town and hired two more bottles of gas.

At eight o'clock we went over to Paul and Elisabeth, Marks and Spencer Christmas cake in hand. Elisabeth's Dutch daughter Anne-Marie was there with her boyfriend Martin — they lived locally — and Josie, who had driven from Amsterdam.

Everyone had been busy cooking and we snacked on French and Dutch traditional treats all evening, well lubricated by the contents of Paul's wine cellar. We concluded he must still have access to a wholesaler! Paul, the only Frenchman, was outnumbered but all we "foreigners" spoke French as the common language of the house. When he was bored with trying to understand us, Paul could watch the television, which was on full blast at the end of the table. Two programmes seemed to take up the night's viewing. One was a hilarious collection of "bloopers" from all over the world, where it was interesting to see the English subtitled into French, and the other was some sort of anniversary celebration of the Crazy Horse strip club in Paris. It was far more suggestive than anything which would have been allowed on British television and the three men certainly enjoyed parts of it. I was just amazed that women could become so painted and unreal. It seemed impossible that these macabre grinning monsters were made of flesh and blood.

A chance remark from me started a family argument about marriage. Paul was very much in favour if there were any young children involved. The Dutch took a far more relaxed attitude. The law was the same for co-habitees as spouses in Holland, said Anne-Marie.

"Unless you are a prostitute, the man you sleep with each night is your husband," declared Elisabeth. It was obviously what she believed about her partnership with Paul. Both widowed, they felt no need for a formal arrangement. At first sight they were an unlikely couple: the kind little round-faced Frenchman and the tall elegant Dutchwoman. But they were devoted to each other.

At midnight it became 1995. France celebrated: but French television allowed the strip-tease to come to its climactic end before they interrupted the Crazy Horse show. One must have one's priorities right.

We toasted the New Year in champagne and everyone in the room hugged and kissed. It was a good feeling.

79

A blanket of snow transformed the well on our boundary.

Chapter Seven

When I woke up next morning I was aware that while my wrist was gradually getting better one of my boobs was very red and uncomfortable. I thought something must be rubbing and tried to take no notice.

We had brought a digital thermometer with us to measure the temperatures and noted that it was six degrees in the house each morning. Outside the temperatures hovered around freezing point. It was cosy under the 15-tog duvet but even with the gas fires going full blast in the bedroom and kitchen, getting undressed and washed using the basin by the front door was not very pleasant. We had to heat our water in the kettle for washing, washing up and cleaning, and when it came straight out of the tap it was cold enough to take our breath away. Tooth-cleaning could be excruciating.

Jack had constructed a set of hollow fire dogs for the *cantou*, attached to a old computer fan which blew air through them and helped it to circulate in the kitchen. It was a wonderful idea and Paul was much taken with it. Unfortunately, due to the design of the fan, it only worked for a few minutes at a time before the fan motor overheated and cut out. We had innocently thought that there was enough potential firewood in the field and outbuildings to keep us going for a stay of only four days but we had underestimated how voracious the fire would be. Soon we were using unseasoned wood which smoked but had no heat. Paul ticked us off: we were just lining the chimney with carbon and showing our ignorance. We replied that wood was so precious in England that people had coal fires — we were not familiar with the niceties of burning logs. We finally ended up burning some of the worst rickety chairs from the salon which we had originally reprieved. We decided that warmth came before sentiment.

Sometimes we managed to get the kitchen up to ten degrees. Our record was a wonderful 13 degrees. In spite of wearing thermal underwear, two woolly sweaters, quilted salopettes and a bobble hat, I could not get warm. My breast hurt and I was very shivery. I refused to believe I was ill. It was unthinkable that I should waste time being ill at St Paradis, but I had no energy and no enthusiasm to do any of the jobs I had planned so excitedly at home in Cheshire. I forced myself to finish off a curtain to stop the icy draughts coming through the back kitchen door, then chickened out by helping Jack.

We started on the bedroom, which was top of our priorities. It looked so clean and attractive in its peach and white livery — nothing like the original dark and dirty room. With its oak-beamed ceiling it cried out for a traditional approach. The other two bedrooms, which had been "modernised" by the Xaviers, could take a more up to date treatment. We had inherited a number of old pictures in large ornate frames which were out of scale in our English house. Here they were in proportion on the large walls and looked perfectly in keeping. We put up the curtain rails over the two windows and cursed French designers. The wooden rails matched the beams and looked just right but they were quite unnecessarily complicated to install and ideally required the invention of a screwdriver which would go round right-angles. The curtains and frilled muslin lining, which I had laboured over in England, complemented the duvet cover and echoed the colour of the walls. I was delighted. The one incongruous touch was the computer on its black metal stand which was destined to go in the red bedroom when it was decorated. I had not even had the energy to attempt to peel off the wallpaper and suspected that the redecoration would have to wait.

We had bought some more wooden shelves on our previous day's shopping expedition and Jack put them together so that we would have somewhere to store our kitchen utensils and tinned food. We put it in the scullery with the first set of shelves and managed to empty a lot more of the cardboard boxes. St Paradis looked more like home every minute.

After lunch at three o'clock, we decided to explore the bread oven building which was built as a sturdy stone lean-to against the side of the house. It had intrigued us since June and we hadn't had time to open it up during the stay in September. All the doors were jammed solid. At home we had fantasised about what might be in there. Would it be another incredible museum like the attic? From the kitchen the bread oven was a beautifully-built domed structure lined with firebricks which we guessed had been used by other villagers as well as the Xaviers. Ovens of this quality tended only to be found in the larger houses. We had no idea what it would be like from the other side.

There were a number of doors. One at the front was about seven feet up, one at the side we reckoned to have been the height to unload a cart and there were two at the back, one at ground level and the other at what we assumed was hay-loft level. Eventually Jack forced open the door at the front, which had simply been rammed into the granite doorframe and had no hinges or catch. From the top of our light aluminium ladder he could see the expected hay-loft. Armed with a torch he explored it gingerly, testing each foothold. We knew the haylofts in the barn had several holes in their wooden floors.

He shouted to me: "It stops about two-thirds of the way along. It's a good thing I didn't open the high door at the back — I could have had a nasty fall."

He came back for the ladder, pulled it up behind him and used it to climb down the other side. He examined the lower door with the light from the torch. The hinges and door latch were very rusty and refused to budge. I passed him a crowbar and a can of WD40 and he set to work on them. With my weight from the outside and him pulling on the inside we finally got the door open. As the daylight streamed in, we saw that at this end he had not been walking on wooden boards but on the top of the stone-built oven which was covered with loose straw. We also realised that it did not go all the way across the building on the far side. A false step in that direction on straw which covered nothingness could also have led to a horrible accident. The area where we were standing had a window covered with shutters which was not visible from the outside and must have been underneath the ivy growing up the lean-to wall. Two long hand-made wooden cat-ladders hung vertically on the house side of the room and an ordinary wooden ladder was propped up against the oven. Massive oak beams, eight feet long and covered with a shawl of straw, leaned against the far wall. Standing beside them was a crude saw-horse and on the dirt floor were about four fraying wicker chair seats, a broken bucket, stacks of fire bricks and smashed eggshells. Judging by their large size, they must have been laid by owls. To our slight disappointment, there was no crock of gold, but we reasoned that each oak beam was worth several hundred pounds. Cleared up, with the window restored and a power supply fed through from the kitchen, it would make an ideal workshop.

We tried to squeeze through the space behind the bread oven but prudence stopped us going very far. We had to climb up behind the beams and on to what appeared to be brushwood which sagged as we put our weight on it. Jagged stones at the back of the oven stuck out at random to impale us and it was impossible to make out what was on the other side. It looked as though the outer shell of the oven had started to collapse, though the fire bricks inside formed a perfect dome. I held my camera at arm's length and took a flash picture. We would find out when the photograph was developed. We knew something was there because the cart-height door on the side led in to it.

Paul and Elisabeth had invited us for a drink at 6.30pm so we cleaned ourselves up and went over. I was still in pain and feeling very strange. I attributed it to the portable gas fires which I thought smelled very strongly. I was convinced I was suffering from carbon monoxide poisoning but Jack, the scientist, laughed off the suggestion. The house was only too well ventilated, he said. Perhaps I had a temperature?

When we arrived they were already entertaining Michel and his wife, together with some mutual friends from Paris. I had spoken to Michel's wife several times but we had not seen them together since the day we viewed the house and I had forgotten he was her husband. I had a slight problem. All the elderly women in the hamlet wore blue pinafores bought from the local agricultural merchant and I had great difficulty telling them apart. They all had grey hair, sensible shoes and were about 5ft 4ins tall. From a distance they looked identical. We called them the "blue pinnies."

Michel's wife invited us to go round to their home for an *aperitif* the next day and we accepted with pleasure. When they had gone we settled down for a gossip with Paul and Elisabeth.

They told us that our house had been sold to a Dutch family, friends of theirs who had fallen in love with it too. They had been devastated when the sale fell through and although they had subsequently bought somewhere else they still hankered after St Paradis. No-one knew what had gone wrong.

Elisabeth had only been at St Paradis for ten years and she had never met Marguerite.

They said that the Xaviers' furniture had been old and some time after Marguerite's death a dealer had come along with a furniture lorry and taken it all away. That explained a chalked sign on cardboard which I had found in our bedroom saying *"Reservé"*, presumably reserving a prized item for a member of the family. Maybe the straw we had found on the floor everywhere had come from packing cases?

It also explained all our "treasures." We imagined busy men, intent only on acquiring the furniture, emptying all the drawers and contents into the nearest fireplaces, just to get rid of everything. They were not interested in old people's "junk". They had not even bothered to look in the attic, thank goodness.

We asked about Michel and his wife and said how much we liked them. Paul said he and Michel had known each other for 50 years, though they'd become much closer since Paul had moved to St Paradis. We were told that their surname was Vallet: Michel was retired but enjoyed helping with what was left of his farm.

Fuelled by Paul's wine — he kept our glasses constantly topped up — and the pleasure of their company, we talked for hours and left embarrassingly late. I tackled cooking my first proper meal with the new gas cooker and learned straight away that grilling wasn't its strong point. The grill was not adjustable. It was either on or it wasn't. There was also the overpowering smell of a cooker being used for the first time. Fried dust? Roast paint? It permeated everywhere. Eventually we had some pork chops which were, well, interesting... At midnight.

Next day my breast was taking on the dimensions of a throbbing red football. There was nothing we could do. It was a public holiday weekend and we were not registered with a doctor. I could hardly take it to the French equivalent of the Casualty Department in the nearest hospital and brandish it at a nurse. I started to swallow paracetamol tablets. A wonky wrist was the least of my problems.

A major consolation was that we had woken up to a wonderland. It had snowed all night and the village was covered in a white blanket. The only vehicle to have made tracks in the virgin snow was a tractor taking fodder to the cattle in a nearby field. We had rarely seen anything so beautiful. It was minus four degrees outside as we tramped round taking photographs before the spell was broken.

Most villagers stayed at home in the warm but the postman got through in his small van. It was the big, shambling man we had met at the *mairie* and we had seen him most mornings. He had faithfully redirected our mail for us since September. He always made a point of coming to the house for a few cheery words whenever he saw we were there, even when he had no post for us: yet another gesture that made us feel accepted in the community. Today he asked if we wanted a calendar — the postman's annual perk in France is to provide a "free" and very informative calendar to his clients who then reciprocate with a little something-or-other. We chose one of the designs on offer in his US Army bag and then fulfilled our part of the bargain. We had a box of chocolates already wrapped for him. Shaking my hand, he said: "I want a kiss, too!" I was glad to oblige. We picked a calendar with oxen on the cover, to remind ourselves of Marguerite's aunt and mother harrowing the Big Wood Field with their *boeufs de labor* in 1915.

We walked down to the Vallets' neat farmhouse and knocked on the door, Mme Vallet opened it and welcomed us in. We gave her their New Year's present of English chocolates and sat, as always in rural France, round the kitchen table. The house was old but hard to date because the exterior had been covered with cream rendering. The floor was concrete and the stairs led straight off the room. The *cantou* had been modernised and was filled by the French equivalent of an Aga, which had fragrant saucepans steaming on the hotplates. Their sheepdog fussed around us while Madame scolded it half-heartedly. We did not know her Christian name and we were of the wrong generation to use it, without a much longer acquaintance. Yet we were comfortable to call Michel by his first name. It was strange: something to do with male bonding as a result of shared work.

They were a couple with complementary virtues. Madame was

quick and bright, ready to chat, delightful and quite sure of herself. She was about the same age as Elisabeth. Michel, aged about 75, reminded us of the Fenlanders in our native Lincolnshire: slow, dignified and capable. He weighed his words carefully. In spite of a heavier accent he was easier to understand than his wife because she often forgot to make allowances for us and sped off with complicated sentences. But with goodwill all round, we managed to communicate quite satisfactorily. We had learned at the beginning that there was no option at St Paradis but to speak French. Apart from Elisabeth, no-one else knew a word of English. If we wanted to survive we just had to get stuck in and forget our embarrassment about making grammatical mistakes. The neighbours didn't mind so long as we tried our best.

Michel had lived all his life at St Paradis — unlike Paul who had only moved there comparatively recently to be with Elisabeth — so he was to be our source of information about the village. We had so much to ask and the Vallets seemed genuinely gratified that we were interested. Since that visit, most of our social conversations with them have been about the "old days."

This time we learned that in its heyday, St Paradis had supported a dairy with 11 workers and a mason with eight employees. Now many of the original houses were empty, including one on the edge of their farmyard.

We were getting into our stride when their son arrived home for his midday meal, so we made our excuses. Madame disappeared into the back kitchen and returned with a box containing four hens' eggs and two ducks' eggs — *au nature*, she assured us. They were enormous. We'd had "proper" eggs during a holiday in the Pyrénées next to a farm where chickens clucked in the yard all day and we knew what a treat was in store. Salmonella? *Pouf!*

We went home and had runny boiled eggs and fresh baguette for lunch: it was delicious. Afterwards we decided to go for a drive.

By now we had agreed that our original DIY plans were impractical. It was too cold to stray far from the fire and I felt awful. We were due to leave the next day and we simply couldn't summon up the enthusiasm to start anything major. This visit, we said, would be devoted to getting to know our neighbours better.

People were more important than decorating: we had a lifetime to do that.

Reversing out of the barn, I had to jump up and down over the back axle of the van before it could get any purchase on the snow. Then we were away. We had decided at the beginning of the trip that we liked the high vantage point in a van: we could see things we'd never spotted from a car. The only problem was that it was right-hand drive and Jack liked to avoid the potholes on his side of the road. This meant that on all the French minor roads my passenger seat was plumb over the white line. I complained frequently but he didn't believe me until he saw some video film I had shot at the time, showing the road from my vantage point. I held my breath and shut my eyes every time a vehicle came the other way. Free of its load, the van handled very well.

Once we had crawled down the lanes, the bigger routes were free of snow. We went through the town and admired all the decorated Christmas trees tied up outside the shops, and set off into the country. It looked glorious. The sky was blue and with below-freezing temperatures the snow was white and crisp. Only the agricultural merchant was open — all the other traders were enjoying their New Year vacation.

On the way home Jack announced that it was his ambition to take the van down the steep snowy hill into St Paradis. The descent started at the cemetery and dropped the height of the church tower into the lane outside the old *auberge*. I thought he was mad but knew better than to argue. If anyone could do it safely, he could. I supposed it was one of those things you did "because it's there." Like climbing Everest without oxygen.

The road was covered with sheet ice and I wondered if we would be joining Marguerite in her ornate tomb a bit sooner than we would have wished. Was the Xavier family vault open to lodgers?

He managed it, of course, slowly and carefully. I was glad we didn't meet the herd of cattle who usually crossed the road from one field to another just at the bend. At the bottom we glided to a halt outside the Echelles and stopped to give the son their New Year present. His mother wasn't there. He invited us in and we had a face-saving conversation which was probably incomprehensible on all sides. I joked about the baby hares: were they big enough for supper yet? He was appalled: they weren't for eating, his mother was looking after them with tender loving care.

We went home and Jack, who was really getting withdrawal symptoms from not doing any DIY, decided to wire up the new pseudo oil lamp which we had chosen to light the bedroom in place of the lightbulb hanging from flex which snaked around the beams and dangled over the bed.

I was suddenly moved to go up into the attic while there was still some light. Marguerite was making my spine tingle again. I took the big torch with me to shine into the corners. I didn't know what I was looking for — anything old and interesting would do. The torch beam picked out a hole in the wall where a stone had been removed. I investigated more closely. Hidden inside was a child's wooden clog, a *sabot*. Had that belonged to Marguerite — or even André? I was drawn to a corner where there were several different baskets on a pile of straw. Some of the baskets contained mouse-nibbled blue socks which I discarded. I wasn't that desperate. Then I saw some paper in the straw and removed it. It was a full colour illustrated brochure advertising hand-driven grain mills like the one on the other side of the attic. It had possibly come with the machine itself. Dates mentioned in the text seemed to indicate that it was about 90 years old. The printing was as clear and sharp as if it had been done the week before.

Jack called to me. He'd heard a knock at the front door. It was Madame Echelle with a bottle of champagne in her hand as a reciprocal present for the chocolates. I couldn't help feeling that she had done rather badly out of the deal.

I invited her in and excused the fact that I was in my salopettes and woolly hat: I was still shivery and cold. I had taken my bra off and was droopy one side and pulsatingly rotund the other. I hoped she wouldn't notice. At least there was no sartorial snobbery in St Paradis, you wore what was comfortable. And in some cases it was obvious that things had been comfortable for a very long time.

Madame Echelle was the easiest of all to chat with and I always got the impression she was glad of some female company. She'd already told me that she had eleven children and two dozen grandchildren. Several grown-up sons were still at home and she looked after them devotedly — rather like the baby hares. She told me that since the death of her beloved husband she had only been able to sleep a couple of hours each night. She spent most of the time in the small hours roaming round the house in search of jobs to distract her. A tear came to her eye at the thought of her husband and I felt deeply sorry for her in her nocturnal loneliness.

She said she was keyholder for the church and promised to give us a conducted tour whenever we wished. It was beautiful from the outside and I made a mental note to take her up on this. I showed her the *sabot*: she remembered them from her own childhood and suggested that a museum might be interested.

I asked about Marguerite. Yes, she recalled her as an elderly lady. After her marriage Marguerite had moved into the next *département* and in her old age only came to St Paradis occasionally. The house had been empty for long periods. Mme Echelle confirmed that Marguerite was buried in the cemetery but was vague about a photograph. There was no name on the grave, she agreed.

After a couple of hours' gossip, and several glasses of Calvados, Mme Echelle left to prepare her sons' supper. I had a new lease of life. She had cheered me up and renewed my faith in my ability to speak French. It was funny how some people made me tongue-tied while others stimulated me to reasonable fluency. I went upstairs and painted the green bedroom floor with woodworm killer.

Next morning the packing was painless. Instead of creating a jigsaw in the back of a car, Jack could just put the suitcase and the few tools we wanted into the cavernous emptiness of the van. It took about ten minutes. While he was doing that, I measured up the front door, back door and door to the stairs so that I could make some more curtains. The one we'd put up to stem the draughts through the kitchen door had been extremely successful. The only snag was that you had to sit in exactly the right place at the pine table or else all the other arctic draughts got you instead. An insulated kitchen would be heaven.

Before we left we asked Paul if he could buy us some firewood.

It came in multiples of four cubic metres which cost about 600F. We tried to give him the money but he wouldn't take it. "Pay me when you come next time," he said. We had already decided that "next time" would be the end of February. Jack had to take all his annual holiday by March 1 and we could manage another short stay. Four days had been better than nothing, but tantalisingly few.

We allowed ten hours to get back to Le Havre and left at 11.30am. At 2.30pm I couldn't stand the discomfort any longer. We pulled up in a lay-by and I rang the doctor's surgery in England. I made an appointment for the following afternoon. At least that would be something to look forward to. We drove all the way from St Paradis to Cheshire with me holding the seat-belt away from my poor chest with my bad wrist.

When I did go to the doctor he diagnosed mastitis — something I hadn't had since the boys were babies — perhaps caused by the seatbelt rubbing on the bumpy outward journey. When I went to bare my boobs he rushed to pull down the surgery's Venetian blinds "so the neighbours in the flats opposite can't see".

As I pulled up my thermal vest I replied: "I can't imagine them hanging out of the windows to get an eyeful of this. It's not a thing of beauty."

He looked and agreed.

Antibiotics did the trick.

Behind the crucifix we saw a tractor being worked in the field.

Chapter Eight

Late February was an anxious time. French seamen were striking and demonstrating against a foreign crewed freight-carrying ship run by one of the operators as well as flexing their muscles before their latest pay deal. Channel crossings were being cancelled and delayed. The seamen and port workers were burning tyres at the most popular seaports and having a wonderfully Gallic series of *manifestations*. There was a fair chance that we wouldn't make it to St Paradis on the ferry we had booked and Jack had no flexibility over his holidays. We were getting a good share-holders' discount on the P&O tickets but a condition of this was that the specifications and dates could not be changed.

Before we left home we rang the ferry company. Was the service between Portsmouth and Le Havre still sailing? We were told that the Dover–Calais route was severely disrupted but received assurances that ours was OK, though circumstances might change at any time. We decided to go ahead. We had nothing to lose but the petrol. The car was packed full of luggage as always and we had to leave behind some pictures and cushions that I had planned to take to the house.

After the usual frustrations on the M6 — always the worst part of the whole journey — we arrived in Portsmouth at 9.30pm only to join a massive traffic jam at roadworks on the inner relief road. We could see the ferry terminal but we couldn't reach it. Our hearts sank as time ticked by. If the ship was on schedule, we might just miss it, regardless of what the French seamen were doing. When we finally made it to the terminal we saw that the Brittany Ferries section was deserted except for a few pickets but there was an enormous queue for our ferry company's checking-in booths. Instead of the usual quick transaction it was taking several minutes for each vehicle to be processed. An employee came along with a printed sheet of paper which he passed through the window. It said that the French industrial action was expected to get worse over the weekend, were passengers sure they still wanted to go?

When we eventually crawled up to the window of the booth, I

asked what was taking so long. The young woman told us that the majority of the passengers were going on a special-rate weekend away: the company could not guarantee to get them back on Sunday. She was having to explain this very carefully to everyone. The universal reaction, she said, had been "whoopee!" No-one had entertained second thoughts — they all wanted to be stranded in France for a bit longer than a weekend break. She said she thought we wouldn't have any problems: we were coming back midweek and the strike should be sorted out by then.

After a calm crossing we left Le Havre at 7.30am and stopped an hour later at our usual breakfast halt off the autoroute in Normandy. The establishment did a roaring trade with travellers and we were ashamed that as "veterans" we enjoyed listening to the English tourists asking haltingly for the different ingredients of their breakfast menus. We had found that owning St Paradis had changed our attitude to being in France. We'd never liked being tourists and we had been shy about using our French too. If we were with French friends we let them do anything complicated on our behalf. Now we were French householders and tax-payers. We had sunk our savings into the French economy, we were accepted in our community even though we knew most neighbours referred to us as "Les Anglais", and we had to fight our own battles. We could not hide behind English-speaking French friends who would rescue us from awkward situations. Though this was daunting it was also liberating. We had to jump in the deep end, relax and teach ourselves to swim. There was no alternative.

We arrived at St Paradis in the late afternoon and once again were welcomed by the warm glow of a log fire which Paul had lit in the *cantou*. This time we knew we would not have to rely on burning the furniture. Before going out to the barn to see our logs, we looked at the digital thermometer which Jack had left behind. It recorded maximum and minimum temperatures, indoors and outdoors. The minimum on the kitchen window-ledge outside had been -9.8 degrees, the minimum inside, 2.1 degrees. At least we knew that in spite of severe provocation, the interior did not freeze. The granite walls acted like a huge insulator: keeping the house relatively warm in winter and cool in summer.

We unpacked and looked in the barn. Stacked neatly at the back of the central part were our four cubic metres of wood, sawn off in identical half-metre lengths. The pile was waist-height, eight or nine feet wide and four feet deep. Paul had heard us arrive and joined us as we admired it. He was upset, the wood had cost more than he had quoted us. We assured him that it didn't matter, we were just delighted to have it and we would give him the money in a minute. It had been seasoned for seven years, he said, and was very good quality. Michel had collected it with his tractor and trailer and he, Paul had stacked it so lovingly. It was a work of art, like a dry stone wall, and we were humbled. He was almost 80! It must have taken him hours. What had we done to deserve such a good friend?

We went back into the kitchen and Jack got out his wallet. How much did we owe Paul? Seventy thousand francs, he answered. We blanched. Nearly ten thousand pounds! Surely not. Perhaps he had said seven thousand francs? That was bad enough — almost a thousand pounds! We couldn't afford it. We hadn't even got that much with us. We checked again. Had he said "seventy thousand francs"? Yes, indeed, said Paul, rather disconcerted. He was most apologetic that it was more than he'd thought originally. People were greedy nowadays. We asked ourselves, just how many years would this wood last? Was it a longterm investment? It was a financial catastrophe. But Paul had paid for it out of his own pocket and we were honour-bound to pay the money back immediately. We would have to raid our emergency French bank account, empty a few English ones and live on baguettes for years with no more home improvements.

Jack put his wallet away and delved for his chequebook. He found a pen and wrote down the figure on the back of an envelope before he filled in the cheque. Was that right? Paul started to laugh. No, no — far too much. But seventy thousand...? *Anciens francs*, explained Paul. Old francs. Abolished in the 1960s because inflation had made the figures so enormous but still the currency of elderly people, who spoke of it as naturally as English pensioners still referred to shillings and pence. One new franc was worth a hundred old ones. We owed him 700 new francs — about £95. We paid cash.

Before we went over for our now ritual visit to Paul and Elisabeth, we lit the portable gas fires in the kitchen and bedroom. Then we unmade our bed and installed a new fleecy electric blanket over the mattress to augment the 15-tog duvet. The two hot water bottles, a Christmas present from Jack's half-sister and her husband, had been lifesavers, but we each had to decide if we wanted warm feet or a warm back. Now we could be toasted all over. The prospect was bliss.

Elisabeth was pleased to see us when we joined her at the kitchen table and we were delighted to see her. She had a special place in our hearts. While Paul was like a cuddly father-figure, she was a loved and respected mother-substitute. We had struck up an instant rapport over the New Year. She called me *"ma petite"* which, for a 47-year-old wearing size 18 clothes, was a nice endearment. We chatted about the strikes and the voyage, ate squares of Dutch cheese and drank copious amounts of Paul's wine. He would have been very offended if we hadn't.

We learned that they were busy entertaining some guests over the next few days, so we invited them for supper on our last night after the visitors had left.

Back home, we stoked up the log fire and ate a pizza we had bought en route at Orléans where we always broke the journey at a hypermarket to do some basic food shopping and have a rest. I was cold, but not shivery and frozen to the core. I realised how ill I'd been in January. If I'd been in Cheshire I would probably have taken to my bed for a few days and enjoyed being waited on. Full of energy now, I couldn't wait to get started. The seasoned wood was giving out a good heat and when I'd aired the salopettes I was comfortably warm. I felt like a new woman.

While Jack worked downstairs I went up to the red bedroom, determined to make a start. I had bought the cream paint for the walls at the same time as the matt peach for our bedroom, and a pretty border which matched the curtains, and I was impatient to transform the room into our study. The only slight problem with my original plan was that I was becoming more aware of the fact that in rural France, everything happens round the kitchen table. Our friends would not expect to be entertained upstairs in comfortable armchairs.

I sprayed the red wallpaper with hot soapy water and waited for it to attack the pre-war glue. The two outside walls were a doddle. The paper lifted off them in satisfyingly large sheets. I was glad it was winter. In the summer the torn bits of paper had harboured some impressive black spiders who probably thought they had a longer claim to residence than we did. I was getting complacent when I tackled the internal walls. They were made of hollow man-made bricks rather than solid granite, and the paper clung tenaciously to the plaster. Though the outside walls were not damp, they had been sufficiently cold over the years to have developed different characteristics.

The wallpaper on the external walls had come off in swathes. The paper on the internal ones came off in postage-stamps. It wasn't long before I was very bored. We decided to call it a day and go to bed. It felt almost decadent to snuggle into the roasting space between the bottom sheet and the duvet: it was possibly the first time since the house was built in 1806 that the occupants had gone to bed in February without a shudder. Even a warming-pan has its limitations.

Chris and Linda had given me a Victorian-style clock for my birthday in January and the following morning we hung it up in a prominent place in the kitchen. Time didn't really matter at St Paradis, but it was interesting to note what it was in theory. We have never managed to make our body clocks coincide with those of *la France Profonde*. Country people get up early, eat at midday, make maximum use of the light, have their supper at about 7pm and go to bed early ready for a 6am start. We are not "morning people." Left to our own devices, we wake at 9.30am, have lunch at 2pm, work until we are too hungry to continue and dine any time from 8pm to 10.30pm, according to how interested we are in what we are currently doing. We go to bed at about 1am. This has given us an unearned reputation in St Paradis for working even harder than we do. Paul will proudly tell his friends: "I got up to have a pee at 1am and their lights were still on. What workers!" They don't realise that when our shutters are closed at 9am we are not conserving the heat in the house and beavering away in the background. We are asleep.

This late rising has an associated problem. By the time we have got up, washed, bought the bread at the town *boulangerie*, had our breakfast, done the dishes and generally pottered about, we can often set off for a nearby town to do some shopping or visit someone like the bank manager or the electricity company. We invariably arrive five minutes after everything has closed for the long French lunch break and we have to wander round for two hours pretending to look in shop windows. We never learn. We have been doing this for twelve years and will undoubtedly do it for the next twelve. We are always going to get up early tomorrow. And we never, ever, do.

This time we were lucky. We needed some things in the nearest city but our chosen DIY store was open at lunchtimes. We were so pleased with the way the wooden shelves were solving our storage problems that we wanted to get two more sets. We had bought an elderly second-hand microwave for £35 and needed somewhere to put it, and I had brought even more kitchen equipment from home. From the culinary point of view, St Paradis was as well-equipped as our house in England, but I enjoy cooking in France and I have roughed it often enough in rented holiday accommodation to know that there is just no substitute for the right tool for the job. We also wanted to put French plugs on all our electrical items — for future reference and for practical reasons. We had two bargain extension flexes bought in France, with very long cables which would stretch round most of the house from the socket in the kitchen. They naturally had French fittings.

Back from the city in the late afternoon, it was time to get out the cordless screwdriver and set to work. The first job was to assemble a sturdy pine work-bench which Jack had bought in an English DIY merchant's sale for £4. It was an incredible bargain, particularly as it all fitted together perfectly. He left it in the kitchen where he had made it and used it to help him put together the shelf units. He sawed up some spare chipboard to make extra shelves, one of which was specially strengthened to take the microwave. While I stacked things on the shelves — one in the kitchen and the other in the scullery — he turned to the IKEA wine-rack components we had brought from home. We are great fans of IKEA but this was a pig to assemble and must have taken a couple of hours. Eventually we put it in the scullery and laid five wine bottles on it. There was space for 40 and they looked rather lonely. We put our duty-free bottles of spirits alongside to keep them company.

Then I discovered how effectively sawdust adheres to carpet tiles.

It had been raining, so while I scratched away at the wretched red wallpaper, Jack tackled some leaks we had found in the barn roof. He was worried about them. A rotten beam in the barn was the only serious structural defect in the whole property but he could not deal with it on his own. It required major surgery. Now he was just metaphorically applying some Elastoplast.

The next day we had a visit from the *maire*, his deputy (*adjoint*) and Paul. The maire was electioneering, canvassing every house in the commune. He had been to see Paul, who had automatically brought him over to us. We didn't have a vote, so it was just a social call. Naturally he was interested to see what we had done to the house. He had known it all his life. After polite refusal all three accepted large glasses of Irish whisky and we chatted about village pump politics. The *maire* we knew, but we had not met the *adjoint* before. He was a young man who introduced himself as an agricultural contractor. He had dark hair and an attractive face. We could understand him, too, which was a bonus. It was mostly the older people who had the impenetrable accents. We made a mental note that he could be useful to know.

When they had gone, I returned to the red bedroom. I had managed to get most of the wallpaper off the internal walls but was having to make repeated assaults on the ornamental borders, which were stuck fast top and bottom. It was very frustrating. Cleaning some black mould off the top of an outside wall, I brushed against the pink ceiling and found my boiler-suited arm covered with pink dust. The walls were bare plaster, well over 100 years newer than the cruder finish in our bedroom and probably contemporary with the wallpaper. I could imagine Marguerite's mother commissioning both jobs at once. I groaned. I had heard it was impossible to paint over distemper, and I needed to paint the ceiling white before I did the walls cream. I tried to wash it off and it spread in a pink gunge. We only had one more full day: there would not be time to wash the distemper off or stabilise the ceiling and then do the rest of the job. I abandoned it. I wanted to do something creative, something that would make a difference to the house. I moved everything out of the scullery and painted it brilliant white. The emulsion went on like a dream, even over the roughest patches, and I had no problems. The whole job was done in an afternoon. When I had finished it looked brilliant. And very white. I put a vase of daffodils in the window and a rug on the floor then I took lots of "after" pictures. Like the bedroom, it was transformed. Its character had not been lost, but enhanced.

I had an overwhelming feeling that Marguerite wasn't too bothered about the red bedroom becoming a study — an alien concept to a farmer's wife — but as a typical proud Frenchwoman she wanted her back kitchen to be clean and fresh again. I found myself thinking sneakily that she "helped" with jobs she approved of and sabotaged the ones that bored her. I had no experience of ghosts but I knew that something of her remained in the house and that it communicated with me. It wasn't frightening — it was a nice feeling. I never felt alone at St Paradis.

While I was busy decorating, Jack had put new locks on the barn doors. Paul was very security-conscious and had pleaded with us to make the place impregnable. Once it became known that the formerly empty house was furnished but unoccupied for long periods, it might become a target for burglars, he thought.

Afterwards Jack wired up a power socket from the fusebox straight up the wall into our bedroom above. It was exactly where we wanted to connect a bedside lamp and our electric blanket, not to mention an extension flex which could be used for the first floor without having wires snaking up the stairs from the kitchen. We had a ceremonial "plugging in".

The following day we were well into our stride. The weather was gorgeous — bright, warm and sunny, a sign of Spring to come. We dressed neatly and drove down to the town to try and sort out our local taxes (*taxe fonçière* and *taxe d'habitation*). We knew that part of the money we had paid the *notaire* at the time of purchase was the equivalent of the British rates but we suspected that this only covered the period from the date of the sale on July 29 to December 31, 1994. We wanted to be model citizens in our adopted country and we didn't want to be accused of tax evasion. We had received no bills for 1995 and were worried in case we had fallen through the net, to be discovered and prosecuted later. We had written to make an appointment with the Public Treasurer for that morning. We arrived with our file of legal documents and announced ourselves. The woman who dealt with us at the counter said the *Trésor Publique* wasn't in: he was on holiday. We wondered if he couldn't face us and had gone on holiday deliberately to avoid a complicated conversation with a crazy English couple who actually wanted to pay their taxes. Such a sentiment was unprecedented... Assured that we would not be put in prison, we arranged to come back during our next visit in June.

We returned via the cemetery. It was beautifully maintained by the commune and had recently been enlarged. A high wall surrounded it, broken by a pair of imposing wrought-iron gates. I had brought my camera with me to take shots of the Xavier family tomb and close-ups of the photographs on the memorials. Apart from being curious I had one of my strange "Marguerite-compulsions" that I should have the portraits on display in the house. However, I was troubled: the more I looked at the picture of the plain young woman in the traditional bonnet and old-fashioned dress, the more I was uncertain about it. This did not seem to be the person who was putting thoughts in my head. She seemed to be the wrong generation to be married to the twinkly-eyed man who gazed out from Henri's memorial.

I looked harder at the whole edifice with its glass covering. Hanging round the sides were the usual votive crucifixes with messages. One read "In memory of my mother". This could not be right. Alain had died long before his mother. It must have been put there by Marguerite for her own mother. The photograph must show Mme Xavier, the woman who kept the farm going while her husband was fighting in the First World War, not Marguerite, the daughter. Had she died young? An inscription said that the perpetual concession for the family tomb had been granted in 1919. They would hardly have been likely to have had it constructed on the offchance that someone might need it. Was Marguerite's father, who had died in 1961, also buried there? Who else was interred without a name? Perhaps the presence of all the Xaviers was taken for granted: Henri and Alain, of course, were not Xaviers.

We were getting into the car in the parking area in front of the cemetery when, behind the village crucifix, we saw a tractor being worked in the field across the road. There was a shout and the tractor stopped. A man in overalls jumped out, waved and ran towards us. It was the agricultural contractor we had met with the *maire* the day before. We shook hands and I explained what we had been doing. Oh yes, he remembered Madame from the days when he was a child. She had been very religious. He was sure she was buried in the cemetery. We chatted a little about his work on the council, wished each other a good day and he went back to his tractor. We were amazed and gratified that someone would actually go to all that trouble just to say "hello." He could easily have put his head down and kept on working.

Back home, I got out my brush and painted the remaining rectangle on our bedroom wall with some matching pink paint we had brought with us. Then I went round the back kitchen touching up places where a second white coat was needed. Jack put on some protective clothing and treated the former jungle area with strong weedkiller in an attempt to discourage growth during the Spring.

We had some lunch and forged on. Jack put a new lock on the front door: the old one had gone wrong several times during this trip, fortunately locking us in rather than out. We insulated the water pipes, did some plastering and made a handrail for the stairs by threading large diameter rope through eyes that had been screwed into the wall so that Paul would have something to hold on to when he paid his daily visits to the house. We had been worried that he might stumble and fall if he ventured upstairs without opening the shutters or switching on the electricity at the mains. The stairs were not very regularly spaced and could trip up the unwary.

We were looking forward to repaying the hospitality of Paul and Elisabeth and determined to make everywhere look as good as possible for when they arrived. We valued Paul's praise and he was always keen to find out about all the jobs we'd done. He took a fatherly pride in our achievements and was especially delighted if we had taken his advice. We usually did.

I prepared a chicken casserole with lots of fresh vegetables, defrosted a bought gateau and laid out a selection of cheeses. We were ready and excited. I wanted to show them that I was a reasonable cook as well as a dab hand with a paintbrush.

A little after the appointed time we heard a knock. I opened the door and was horrified to find them on the doorstep, leaning arm-in-arm looking very grimfaced.

"Something terrible has happened," said Elisabeth and started to cry. We ushered them inside.

"Paul went to sleep in the sunshine this afternoon and when he woke up he was blind," she said.

The family had arranged for him to go to the doctor the next day.

We hugged them both and sat them down at the table. Naturally enough neither was hungry and we immediately lost our own appetites. Elisabeth cut up Paul's small serving and helped him to put it on his fork.

She told us that Paul had cataracts. He had been reluctant to have anything done about them because his brother had undergone simultaneous cataract operations on both eyes and had lost his sight. The brother had been fiercely independent and had carried on living at home with help from various people. Then one day he had decided to use the gas cooker and had set himself on fire. He had burned to death. The first they had known was when they heard a newsflash on the local radio. The memories upset her and she began to weep again.

They left as soon as it was polite to go and we helped them back to their house in the darkness. We were equally upset. Paul squeezed every ounce of enjoyment out of life. He and Michel were like characters from "The Last of the Summer Wine" television series. His one goal in life was to be useful to others. If he was blind all his pleasures would be taken away. He would not be able to cope with being dependent.

While we were packing up the next morning we saw members of the family coming and going, and Paul being driven away. He returned later. We did not interfere. When it was time to leave, we went across and embraced them. I held Elisabeth's hand. "What has happened?" I asked.

"The doctor says he has a detached retina. He has got to go into hospital tomorrow to have an operation. He will be in for five days," she replied miserably. "He is 80 next week. What about the anaesthetic..?" She was distraught and Paul was being brave. For the first time, he looked old and lost. We comforted them both as best we could and promised to keep in touch.

We left St Paradis in a sombre mood and shed some tears ourselves.

As soon as we got back to England we bought a 'get well' card in a South Coast supermarket and posted it off with a special message inside. Then a couple of days later we bought a birthday card and sent that too, hoping that someone would have telephoned if something awful had happened to Paul under the anaesthetic. We consoled ourselves that he really did have the heart of an ox.

Shortly afterwards a letter arrived from Elisabeth. Paul was fine. The operation had been a complete success and Paul had been delighted with our cards. He was looking forward to going back to the house and opening our shutters. And perhaps a little gardening might be in order..?

It was wonderful news.

Chapter Nine

We were really excited. Alex and his fiancée Michelle had taken up our offer to come to St Paradis for the first week of our two-week holiday in June. Apart from the fact that we were delighted that they would be visiting the house for the first time, Jack urgently needed Alex's strength and practical skills to help him repair the rotten beam in the barn. We dare not let it deteriorate any longer.

Our aim this time was to mend the roof and then tackle the bathroom. I was geared up to painting the study at last. We had bought a pine bed-frame for Alex and Michelle to go in the green bedroom and Jack had made a matching bedside cabinet. They had said they didn't mind sleeping in a peeling pre-war decor. There was no electricity in there but we had an extension flex and lots of romantic candles.

We had got hold of some long pine beams and bought a big aluminium ladder of our own — much lighter than the monster we had borrowed from Mme Echelle's son. We bought a roof rack for Alex's Peugeot and packed all the long items on it. We shared the luggage between the two cars and prepared to leave. Alex went home to pick up Michelle, who had been working.

Now, as I've said, Jack is a wonderful man 99.9 per cent of the time, except before a ferry journey. When the magic hour for leaving had come and gone he was so worried about missing the boat that he decided to set off for Portsmouth and leave Alex to find his own way. Jack argued that Alex had a fast car and would surely catch us up.

As an anxious mother I kept my counsel but worried. Alex and Michelle did not catch us up. I had written precise instructions for them in case we got separated but there was always the chance that they had missed a turning somewhere. Most of the journey was by motorway. Perhaps they were following the wrong one? The implications of it all made me feel sick. Would we ever find them again?

We stopped to use the loos at a new service station on the M42. I stayed in the car while Jack went into the building first. We had

Jack and Alex repaired the barn roof and beams.

parked so that we had a view of the carriageway. Then I saw a familiar grey car topped with ladders and wood forging past at considerable speed. They had only been one minute behind. They should be easy to catch up.

Unfortunately we had reversed roles. Instead of us going steadily at the front, hoping Alex and Michelle would catch us, we were now at the back and they were going faster and faster, getting more panicky when they could not find us. We in turn had to speed up. The journey became like a bizarre motor race, which each car's occupants trying to overtake the other. Alex's Peugeot had more horsepower than our Cavalier.

On the outskirts of Portsmouth, four hours after we left home, we were astounded to find Alex pulling in behind us, flashing his headlights and gesticulating. Where had he come from? We hadn't overtaken him. He followed us to the ferry terminal and when we were both parked in our lanes we got out for a rather frosty post mortem. Alex thought we had evaded him for the full 230 miles and was cross with me for giving them an unintentionally misleading instruction near Southampton. We told him we had been chasing him for 100 miles. If he hadn't had that "diversion" at Southampton which had taken him round in a circle we would not have met up at all. This did not augur well for a 370-mile journey in France the next day.

We left Le Havre at 7.30am and drove in convoy to our breakfast stop in Normandy. We kept together as far as the hypermarket in Orléans. We were in formation when we had a picnic lunch in an autoroute lay-by. We stuck together as far as the city nearest to St Paradis, where we bought a double mattress for Alex and Michelle. We strapped it carefully on top of his roof-rack and watched it like hawks in our rear-view mirror in case it flipped up. Alex followed us up to the front door at St Paradis at 5.30pm. We had not been more than a couple of hundred yards apart for seven hours of driving. It was an amazing tribute to French roads.

We had a quick look round. The grass in the field had been cut and it looked neat and cared for. We unpacked, ate some pizzas and introduced Alex and Michelle to Paul and Elisabeth. Paul said

Georges had cut the hay. After a chat and the usual glasses of wine with our neighbours, we put the bed together and gave the youngsters a conducted tour.

Michelle doesn't like spiders. She can't help it. She has a thing about them. Especially big black ones. We had sworn there weren't any spiders left at St Paradis: we were telling the truth, we certainly hadn't seen any in February. But this was balmy June and the old house and its land were teeming with life. There were no black spiders but there were lots of thin-legged brown field spiders. They were living in the wallpaper in the green bedroom.

It must have been about eight o'clock when Alex and Michelle started to strip the paper. This was a job for which I had mentally allocated at least a couple of full days, given how hard the wallpaper had stuck to the internal walls in the adjoining red bedroom. It was something I was going to get round to during another trip.

We could tell by the sound effects when Alex was acting as executioner. Each wallop was preceded by a scream.

By about midnight they had stripped off enough of the peeling paper for Michelle to feel sufficiently comfortable to go to bed. I was full of guilt. I loved the house so much that I had overcome my dislike of its "wildlife". Clad in a boiler suit and gloves I could face anything. What anguish were we inflicting on our dear future daughter-in-law? Would she ever come again? We had bought the house for her, too.

We set up an ultraviolet "insectocutor" in the kitchen to zap the enemy as it came over the threshold and put another in the green bedroom. Creepy-crawlies, be warned!

Next day we went back to the city in both cars to stock up on food and buy all the components to make up the bathroom. This was serious shopping. We had put quite a lot of money on one side, had drawn detailed plans and were looking forward to making the house civilised. Once we had a bathroom we could invite people outside the immediate family to stay. We could not ask them to get washed at the kitchen sink, which was the current state of affairs.

In one of the big *bricolages* (DIY superstores) we found exactly what we wanted at special bargain prices: a beige bathroom suite comprising lavatory, washbasin, bidet and galvanised bath, with matching marbled wall tiles and some attractive light brown floor tiles. I'd made the curtains in advance and everything co-ordinated. We threw in all the associated taps and shower attachments. Then I realised with a sinking heart that the tiles alone were incredibly heavy. They were stacked on a special trolley which I could hardly shift, let alone steer. Jack seriously doubted if we could get all our purchases into the two vehicles without doing the suspensions a serious injury. But another 50-mile round trip was not inviting, so we shoved everything in and hoped for the best. The bath went upside-down on Alex's roof-rack and made interesting music as he drove home.

We unloaded it all into the cow byre part of the barn and left it in its cardboard boxes. Then after supper, Alex and Michelle returned to finish their wallpaper stripping.

It was Sunday the next day. We went down to the town to buy some fresh bread. After breakfast Jack and Alex inspected the barn and started to take off the roof tiles in the affected area. Elderly villagers had told us once that the roof was "new". Except where we had the problem, it certainly appeared to be in excellent condition and we thought it was probably about ten years old. We even wondered if it might be covered by a guarantee. Jack looked at a tile he had removed. It had been made in the next village in 1929.

The cement flashing covering the join between the wall and the roof had crumbled away and was allowing water to run down the wall. Over the years rain had dripped on to one of the major beams spanning the length of the barn and the damp had made it rotten at the end which fitted into a socket in the wall of the house. The affected part would need to be cut off and replaced with a piece of oak the same size, "splinted" on to the sound end of the original beam. A third problem was that the water had also rotted a beam supporting the slope of the roof against the wall, so that the central section had fallen away. This thinner beam would have to be replaced in its entirety. The unaccustomed weight of the sagging roof tiles in this area had distorted the battens to which the tiles were nailed. These would have to come off and be renewed, too. It was a big job. The men relished the prospect.

With the power turned off at the mains, Michelle and I started to tackle the removal of the crude and worrying electrical wiring in the green and red bedrooms. Another priority this visit, along with the barn and the bathroom, was to do as much rewiring as possible.

Cloth-covered pre-war aluminium wires ran inside wooden conduits up the walls, along the edges of the ceilings and emerged to be tacked naked across the ceilings to light-bulbs or dangle down the walls to switches which must have hung over beds. Here and there they were repaired with tape where they were at their most lethal. More modern wiring leading to fluorescent strip lights downstairs ran in grey plastic conduits: upstairs this must have been the original stuff from the exciting days when electricity came to the Limousin. The miracle of light must have been more important than the aesthetics of its installation. The light sockets were black bakelite and the wall switches were white china. They were far too dangerous to leave as sentimental reminders of earlier days.

The wooden conduit was held in place with nails, often driven to within a hairsbreadth of the live wires inside.

Wearing gloves to avoid splinters, we yanked the conduit off the walls and prised its stubborn bits away with screwdrivers. Its path could be traced round the rooms from the pathway of nail-holes we left behind.

After a thorough reconnoitre of the barn, Jack and Alex went up into the attic to see how easy it would be to take up the floorboards. The new wiring could then be run between the attic floor and the false ceilings in the red and green bedrooms. Alex, less patient than his father, hauled them up with leverage from a big crowbar. The oak boards groaned with the strain as they were disturbed for the first time for nearly 200 years. They were an early version of tongue and groove, and the gaps where they did not meet had been filled with pieces of wood cut to exactly the right size. There was more to the dirty floor than met the eye.

Jack and Alex wanted to get at two specific areas of floor and to negotiate the way over the place where an interior wall divided the two bedrooms. The floor needed to be clean and clear of obstructions. I put on my overalls and started to move things out of the way, sweeping up as I went. I moved a large pile of sawn oak planks from one side of the attic to the other, together with some articles which looked like wicker stretchers. Mme Echelle had told me they were used for drying prunes in the bread oven.

I idly asked Marguerite if she had anything interesting up there to show me. In a barrel of rubbish I found a very old and damaged prayer book, where the "s's" were printed like "f's." Searching for the other *sabot*, my eye was caught by something white tucked into a space between the eaves and the top of the stone wall of the house. I pulled it out. It was a lower jawbone, and there was another the same a foot or two away, almost hidden inside the fabric of the building. My knowledge of anatomy was not good enough to tell if the bones had belonged to sheep or calves. They were long thin "v"-shapes, with empty tooth sockets. Why would a farming family not only keep such jawbones but apparently hide them away like that? It might not be unusual to find them outside in the barn, but upstairs in an attic was odd. Farmers were not sentimental about their animals: surely one calf or sheep was much the same as another? Was there some country ritual at the bottom of the discovery, or was it all very mundane?

In our eyes a visit to a good builders' merchant is as much fun as a trip to Harrods. On Monday we were looking for old tiles to replace the broken ones in the barn roof. Mme Vallet whetted our appetite. She was picking strawberries in a little garden near Paul's house, which Michel kept cultivated. The land in the village was so rocky that the Vallets' own back yard was not suitable for growing vegetables. She told us about an enormous builder's merchant in a place whose name I couldn't catch, which was full of everything we might ever need, at really low prices. We couldn't resist it. I went back to the garden with a Michelin map of the *département*. Perhaps Madame could point it out on the map for me? We could work out the best route to take. She did not have her glasses and repeated the name slowly with a rather strange look on her face. I discovered the place in question was only about three miles away and there was only one road to it...

We followed her instructions minutely and found nothing to resemble what she had described. But it was early closing and it was — naturally — lunchtime, so perhaps the expedition was doomed. Maybe at 2.30pm a builder's merchant would materialise out of nowhere in all its tantalising glory. We decided to try another day.

We were at the stage of a St Paradis holiday where we didn't really feel like knuckling down to serious work. It happens without fail every time we go, round about the third day. We had major jobs to do but really we just wanted to poodle about enjoying the simple fact of being there. We salved our consciences by finding another builder's merchant. It wasn't the Aladdin's Cave promised by Mme Vallet, but it was cheap and an excellent source of electrical bits. We also found a woodyard which had some wood to replace the battens and just two matching roof tiles. They saw us coming. The tiles cost £2 each but were essential. We paid up.

Back home we guiltily started work. The men began by jacking up the damaged beam to support it while they cut off the rotten end, while Michelle and I started painting the green bedroom. There was still some sort of curse on progress with decorating the red one.

I had wanted to make the spare bedroom as bright as possible. Unlike our bedroom, with its two windows, this only had one — which tended to make it dark. The green wallpaper and borders had obviously once been very pretty but it was a cold colour. I decided that yellow would fill the room with sunshine. In England I had tracked down the exact Dulux shade I wanted and worked out that we needed three cans. Our branch of B&Q was having a sale and they had three cans of the right sunny colour: one in matt, one in soft sheen and one in silk. It was expensive paint and the containers were half-price. We bought them, deciding to paint different walls with different finishes according to how the light struck them.

Michelle had never done any painting before but she is enormously conscientious over every task she tackles. She felt happier with a fairly narrow brush, which made the job longer, but I am sure she didn't have a single run or a spot of paint out of place. She put my more slapdash style to shame. As she worked, the room began to be transformed.

While she did the walls, I went for the ceiling. I'd taken advice about painting over distemper and had been told that it should be all right, despite my misgivings. The brilliant white certainly seemed to go on well over the pink distemper — which had been used on both bedroom ceilings. The room was divided by a boxed-in beam across the centre, so I spent several hours painting the 9ft x 12ft half nearest the window.

I hate doing ceilings. They have to be done but I don't do them with any pleasure. As far as I am concerned, ceilings are a necessary evil which give me a stiff neck. Like the first stage of labour, ceiling-painting is something to be endured on the way to more creative things.

I prepared us a quick supper and afterwards went back to admire my handiwork. I could have cried. The brilliant white was fighting with the dusty distemper and lifting off in big blisters. It would all have to be scraped off, coated with stabliser and repainted. I suppose I had known that all along, really. For the first time, the house had conspired against me.

Jack and Alex had had more luck. They had sawn off the rotten end of the beam and were looking for something to replace it. They had suitable new wood from England but would have preferred something original. Then, Jack says, he had his first flash from Marguerite, that he should try in the bread oven building we had opened up in January. There they found an oak beam with exactly the same dimensions as the one they had cut up. They sawed off the requisite length, fitted it straight into the socket in the wall and splinted it on to the first beam with massive coach-bolts, using English wood as a casing.

Tuesday was a day of hard work. Poor Michelle was learning a lot about painting but not much about the Limousin or even St Paradis. She and Alex had hardly even been out for a walk round the village.

It took me nearly all day to scrape off the awful combination of old distemper and modern emulsion. It couldn't stay as it was, but it didn't want to come off either. Painting on the stabliser was an even more unpleasant job. It was as thin as water and ran from the brush right down my arm, dissolving my rubber gloves into wrinkles. I was furious with myself for not doing a proper job in the first place and took it all in the spirit of a penance.

Michelle, on the other hand, was doing brilliantly. She managed to paint most of the room in its various finishes of yellow — and to remember which wall was which when it came to touching up bits she had missed with paint from the right pot. Even better, she and Alex had lifted off the door, sanded the oak doorframe down to the wood, and also uncovered the wooden battens which supported the wall between the two bedrooms. These oak battens had been covered with wallpaper and in other rooms, similar ones had been painted over by past decorators. Alex and Michelle had had the bright idea of sanding them and varnishing them. They shone a mellow dark brown against the yellow paint and looked beautiful. Michelle had turned out to be a born expert with a belt sander and was justifiably pleased with herself.

Alex's work in the bedroom was done before breakfast. Afterwards he and Jack went out to the barn for a day of fiddly work. They had to take out the damaged small beam which had rotted away and replace it with a new one. The beam they had brought from England was too wide, so they cut it in half lengthwise with a circular saw and joined up the ends so that it was twice as long. Then they inserted it up the inside edge of the roof and attached it to the wall. All this involved a lot of work on a high ladder and Jack had made himself a harness at home in England so that he could be roped up safely.

Wednesday was Jack's birthday: the second he'd spent in the Limousin. We went down to the bread shop together in the morning and stopped off at the paper shop to buy some postcards. I saw that they had a good selection of local books and were displaying a new one, tracing the Resistance in that part of the Limousin. It was the 50th anniversary of the end of the Second World War and bookshops at home had been full of reminiscences about VE Day on May 8. At the time I had felt desperately sad that it was also the 50th anniversary of Alain's cruel and unnecessary death at Theresienstadt. I bought one of the books about the Resistance in the hope that he would be mentioned in it.

At home I examined the book closely. It was fully illustrated and also contained lists of "martyrs" and *résistants*. I could not find Alain anywhere. Then I suddenly remembered that Marguerite and Henri had lived just over the border in the next *département* after their marriage. St Paradis was really Alain's grandparents' home. He had missed on out on his honourable mention by literally a quarter of a mile.

The photographs were heartbreaking. It was hard to know which were the worst: the portraits of men, young and middle-aged, who had had given their lives, shown in smiling photographs submitted by their families; or the pictures of mutilated corpses in their death agony, clinically photographed by the Nazi authorities and filed away for some ghastly future reference. There was no specific mention of Theresienstadt, but some emaciated survivors were pictured after their return from the concentration camps. The book was fascinating but tantalising: Alain had been arrested in late 1943 while he was at University in Clermont-Ferrand and was unlikely to have been involved in what was happening near his home, where much of the activity was centred on sabotage before D-Day and ambushing the German army afterwards. There had been some significant and bloody ambushes not far from St Paradis in August 1944. I could learn an enormous amount about what had happened locally, but almost nothing about his story.

The Resistance had always been split into different groups. There was *Liberation*, which contained many trade unionists and socialists, *Combat*, which was politically more right-wing, the communist *Francs-Tireurs et Partisans (FTP)* and the *Maquis*, which was based on bands of young men who took to the forests and

115

mountains to avoid forced labour in Germany. As a student, it was unlikely that Alain would have been in the *Maquis*.

I analysed the lists in the book to see where the people had died who had been sent to the camps. For many there was just *"mort en déportation"* with no placename or date. The majority had died at Buchenwald, with the rest at Mauthausen, Dachau, Auschwitz and Flossenburg — well before the death marches took place. It was very likely that Alain too, had been at one of these camps. Had any of the men on the roll of honour met him? I could only find one other person described as *"disparu"* and that was at Auschwitz. I wondered about the exact significance of the word. Perhaps, with Alain, it was because the Germans, who were so efficient at accounting for all their victims, had run away the day before he died, so there was no official record. He would also not have been "on the books" at Theresienstadt if he had only just arrived there from another camp. Most of the camps in Central Germany where the other Limousin *résistants* had been deported were within reach of Theresienstadt by a forced march. Even more research would have to be done.

During the day we all worked hard: Jack and Alex on the uncomfortable and awkward job of carefully removing tiles and renewing battens, and Michelle and I on the decorating — in what was now rapidly becoming the "yellow" bedroom rather than the "green" bedroom.

We celebrated Jack's birthday in the evening with *"Chicken à la persil"* and a delicious frozen dessert which was a combination of gateau and sorbet and cost a fortune from the town's tiny super-market. We illuminated the table with candles and asked Jack to blow one out in the traditional manner. We decided it was obviously a patented draught-proof candle because he ran out of puff at the sixth attempt when we were all weak with laughter. We almost had to douse it in a bucket of water!

We had bought a green plastic patio table on one of our shopping expeditions so that we could all sit comfortably round it. When and if we ever had a patio, it could go outside, we reasoned. It was great when covered with a table-cloth — it even looked like a real table then — but we had to be careful not to kick the legs or grab it whilst sitting down because it was liable to tip over. Mealtimes were punctuated with rugby tackles to save the casseroles and vegetable dishes and spilt drinks were commonplace.

When Thursday dawned we were determined to get as much done as possible. Alex and Michelle had decided that the mock-ebony fireplace in the yellow bedroom needed cheering up, so they painted the wooden surround white and the remaining half yellow. Michelle was just painting the window area white and I was tackling the skirting boards when there was a knock at the door and a cry for linguistic help from Jack. Downstairs in the kitchen I saw a person standing by the door in a blue boiler suit. It was almost round, with pink cheeks and short dark hair. For the life of me I did not know whether to address it as *"Madame"* or *"Monsieur."* While I covertly inspected its chin and chest for tell-tale signs of hairs or curves, it asked if it could have permission to put its cows in our field. From the cowpats we had seen in there, we suspected that the cows probably spent quite a lot of time in the field anyway. So to be nice to someone we thought was a neighbour, we agreed, on the proviso that we could have the land back whenever we wanted, as we had plans for a wild garden with a landscaped stream and pond. This was also agreed. We exchanged names and addresses and discovered that the person was a *"Madame"* after all. After she had gone we congratulated ourselves on pleasing another St Paradis stalwart.

In the afternoon we accompanied Alex and Michelle to the city so they could buy Father's Day presents for Jack and Michelle's father and have a break from working. They insisted that they had had a satisfying holiday and that the house was much better than they had expected, but we felt guilty that they hadn't exactly painted the town red.

We bought some coving to go in the yellow bedroom. I had finished the ceiling but the sparkling new paint accentuated the fact that there were shadowy cracks between the false ceiling and the tops of the walls. Coving and a pretty border — which I had brought from home — would finish the job off perfectly.

We had aimed to put the curtains up in the bedroom before they left, though it just wasn't possible. But Alex and Michelle's last night was spent in a bright, sunny room from which spiders had been banished and all trace of 1930s paint had been obliterated. Their duvet cover was of bold primary colours and was basically the same material as the future curtains, which I had trimmed and edged. It was possible to visualise the end result and to be pleased by it. We promised them lots of photographs of the finished product and extracted assurances that they would come back — lots of times — to take advantage of it.

They drove off at 7.45am next day with a set of instructions on how to reach Le Havre. Alex was worried. He said he had just followed Jack all the way to St Paradis without looking at the road signs. They didn't believe us when we said the route was easy. We made sure they allowed eight hours to catch the late afternoon sailing. When we phoned them at home a couple of days later we were appalled to find out that they had taken just over five hours for the whole journey... When we started to fuss we reminded ourselves of my dear father who, when Jack was driving him at 90mph (in the days when it was legal), looked at the tachometer instead of the speedo, saw we were doing 6000 revs and remarked to my mother: "This seems awfully fast for 60mph." We never owned up.

Chapter Ten

$\mathcal{I}$ took Alex's place as the labourer in the barn. We started at 8.30am and finished the job at 8.30pm, absolutely shattered. I hate ladders and much of the day's work entailed carrying heavy roof tiles up an admittedly short ladder so that Jack could deal with them on the high ladder. It was good for the soul.

Jack was deliberately doing the job the wrong way round. A proper roofer would start at the bottom and tile up the roof from the outside. A proper roofer would have all the right ladders and a head for heights: he would be unperturbed about working some 15 metres above the ground. Jack was brave but not stupid. He knew his limitations and we didn't have a cat ladder that was less than 100 years old. So he worked from the inside, downwards, harnessed to a rope which ran over the main beams of the barn and was anchored safely. If he fell, he would dangle embarrassingly over a soft bed of straw, rather than break his neck on the granite in the field. It seemed worth the extra hassle it created.

The frustrating part was rebuilding the cement flashing between the wall and the roof tiles. While I used a pulley to raise the cement bucket to the required height and then held it in position from my ladder, Jack was stuck with his shoulders protruding through the small gaps between the battens. In an ideal world he would have carefully smoothed the cement down with a trowel. Today he had to fling it at the desired spot and prod it. It was an extremely hot day and often the cement dried before he could finish prodding. Heath Robinson would have been proud of us.

At lunchtime we heard a call from below and saw Paul with a middle-aged couple who were waving photographs of our dogs which we had sent to Paul and Elisabeth months before. We climbed down the various ladders and went over for an *aperitif* and a chat, covered in straw, dust and bits of cement. It turned out that the pair were Dutch friends of Paul and Elisabeth, who had a new house nearby which they had "done up" from a basic shell over the past eight years. Their names were Jan and Beatrice and they had two dogs which they adored. They said they were sure

I hung the washing round the back garden: it smelled of heaven.

that as we liked dogs we would all get along very well. We were invited over for a drink the next night and they drew a map on a piece of scrap paper. We chatted in French for Paul's benefit but Beatrice could speak English very well and Jan, though quieter, could understand. They said, in English, that they thought English was a much more sensible language than French. We felt, indeed, that we had a lot in common!

We celebrated the finishing of the roof by taking a detailed video and toasting the achievement with a bottle of sparkling Saumur wine. Immediately after supper, we tottered off to bed.

When I was a child, I remember a high spot of the school holiday weeks was helping my mother do the washing. She had a state-of-the-art Hoover washing machine with an electric wringer. You filled it with water, heated it up, added the detergent until it was satisfyingly bubbly, put in the washing and set the paddle wheel on the side of the machine churning away. If you hadn't put in enough water and you took off the lid to investigate any strange noises, it caught you with a faceful of hot soapy water. My favourite bit was wringing things into the sink without getting my fingers caught in the mangle rollers. I thought, with its hoses and electric switches, that the Hoover was the most sophisticated and beautifully designed machine I'd ever seen.

At St Paradis we also had a state-of-the-art Hoover washing machine. It had belonged to Jack's mother and we had found it in our garden shed in Cheshire. Jack had serviced it and we had brought it over after Christmas. It was the same model as my mother's, circa 1958. We had a startlingly modern accessory for it. My mother's 1970s spin drier.

The reason for the antiquity of the machinery was not pure parsimony on our part. French electricity is charged on various tariffs, according to the amount of current you need to take. St Paradis was on one of the lowest. If we used anything which took much power we would trip the fuses. We intended to upgrade, but not until we had done all the rewiring. So for the time being, a 1950s washing machine was better than no washing machine.

I decided to do my first laundry session the next morning. It was a glorious day and everything should dry quickly, I thought.

The basic design fault was that my mother's machine had had a heater: Jack's mother's was a slightly less posh version, without a heater. So I had to heat the water first. In saucepans and in the kettle. It took about half an hour to get enough water to cover the top of the paddle.

It was the most gloriously messy business, especially the rinsing. I took up the carpet tiles from the concrete floor and let rip. I had not had so much domestic fun for years. We had a twin tub when the children were small and nappy washing loomed large on the daily horizon. Now, as the lazy owner of an automatic machine, I had forgotten just how long it takes to do washing when you have to stand over it. I had forgotten that spin driers leap all over the kitchen unless you lean on them. I had forgotten that all my water was draining out of the hosepipe through the wall and down the lane into our next door neighbour's drive. I created a small dam to divert it back onto our land, and hoped he wouldn't notice.

I left the front door open so that Paul and passing "pinnies" could see just what a wonderful housewife I was. I could drop things into future conversations like: "I was just doing the washing when...."

It took two hours to wash all our bedlinen and a week's worth of clothes. It would probably have taken twice as long with three loads of an automatic washer, except that I would have spent a total of five minutes loading it and five minutes unloading it and would have forgotten all about it for the rest of the time. The minutes spent pegging the linen out on the line would have been the only similar procedure.

I hung the washing round the back garden at St Paradis and when I brought it in it smelled of heaven.

In the afternoon we went to the *départemental* capital to get some DIY stuff and I bought a special flower arrangement to go on Marguerite's grave. I had brought some pretty silk narcissi from England but found them difficult to weight down with pebbles and Oasis in a container and I was concerned that they would not last long. The other "flowers" in the cemetery were of that peculiarly French heavy plastic which looks crude close up but will survive whatever weather is thrown at it. I had been too embarrassed to go into a funeral director's to buy some but found a selection in one of the *bricolages*. I chose a pot of blue crocuses which looked quite realistic and not "over the top" for a gesture from a stranger.

At 7.30pm I was just washing my hair in the sink by the back door, ready to go to the Dutch couple's house, when we had visitors. It was Paul and Georges, the agricultural contractor. Paul announced proudly that while we were in England he had arranged with Georges that he would look after our field in return for having the hay crop. He had cut the field beautifully, hadn't he?

We were horrified. This was exactly the sort of agreement we had wanted but we had given our word to the woman farmer the day before. We explained, appallingly embarrassed. Whatever could we do? We said we had better stick by our original agreement for a year, then Georges could have it. Georges and Paul kept saying it didn't matter, but we knew that it mattered very much. They said the farmer had taken advantage of us: we gathered she was unpopular for snapping up all the available land in the village and putting her cows on it. The animals would ruin the field and we would never be able to make a garden out of it because of the mud and the way the cattle would churn up the land. *Oh la la!* To cap it all, the Fat One had accused Georges of stealing our hay when he cut the field.

Paul was obviously hurt that we hadn't consulted him, our guru. Georges had innocently looked forward to the hay next year. Madame had our agreement that the cows could go on the meadow. Help!

Georges asked us if we could help him to find a part for his English silage baler. We agreed immediately and said we would have a look at it the next day. Perhaps that might pacify him a bit.

We excused ourselves because we were going to be late for our date with the Dutch. We were devastated: what awful sin had we committed? Would we be forgiven? Whatever happened, someone was going to be upset. It was our first *faux pas*.

We found Jan and Beatrice's house. It was beautiful. Jan was a wonderful craftsman, especially with wood, and had done a superb job. It transpired that they had bought the shell of the house from the widow of the owner who had died before he could finish it. They had done exactly the same as us, bringing materials from home and living on a building site for years on end. It had all borne fruit eventually.

They were a delightful couple and we had an instant rapport with them and their dogs: two French Spaniels who reminded us of our Setters in both shape and temperament. We knew that we would become firm friends — and we have. We were astonished to discover that they had been married for 40 years. They did not look old enough.

We sought their advice about the field. "Ask Paul," they replied. "He is a wise and respected man. He knows everything. He will sort it all out for you."

They had some wonderful books of old photographs, showing the Limousin at the turn of the century. Simple country people were pictured in their homes and with all their farm implements. I bored Jan and Beatrice silly by saying "We've got one of those!" and "There are several of them in the attic." One thing worried me — the houses were very primitive inside and many people seemed to live little better than their animals. I hated to think of the Xaviers like that: everything we knew about them pointed to much more sophistication.

Before we left we invited the Dutch back to sample our building site at St Paradis.

I lay awake half the night worrying about the field. For nearly a year nothing had gone wrong with our idyll, now we were in a situation which, judged by life's normal crises, was of negligible importance but might make all the difference to how we were perceived in the village. I was terrified that we might have hurt Paul's feelings irrevocably. After all, we had told him many times that we trusted him to make decisions for us when we were not at St Paradis. And poor Georges, being accused of stealing our hay when all he was doing was helping... I tossed and turned — and agonised. In the morning I confided my worries to Jack. He too had been agonising, but he had come up with a solution.

"At home in England, our word is our bond," he said. "If we have agreed something we can't change it. We're pillars of the community. But here we might just get away with being 'The Stupid English'. We don't want the cattle in the field, do we? We like Georges and we want him to look after it as we had always planned someone should. We just didn't know who to ask.

"So I reckon we grovel to Madame and ask Paul to tell her that we didn't understand that the arrangement had already been made with Georges. We're soft in the head: we don't understand French properly. For all we know, Paul told us that first night and we really didn't understand. I know she's like Mike Tyson, but if we ask Paul to tell her after we've gone home, she can't come and beat us up."

We swallowed our pride, went round to Paul's house and explained to him through Elisabeth what our cover story was. He laughed: "Don't worry your heads about that! It's not serious. I'll tell her, that Fat One." We got the impression he would enjoy doing it.

After that, for the next week whenever we heard a tractor which might be carrying the Fat One, we turned the house lights off and dived under the stairs for cover. Cowards? Of course.

While Jack was busy wiring up new power sockets and lights, I continued with the yellow bedroom, painting the window and fireplace in white gloss and varnishing the door frame. We tried to stick the coving on, but discovered we'd bought the wrong sort of glue. This was annoying as we had put back our first choice in the *bricolage* and been guided by one of the assistants.

I hadn't felt Marguerite's presence much while the children were with us, but she came back when I was working on my own. She seemed to plant messages in my head — usually accompanied by a freezing tingle which started in my spine and spread down my legs.

As I painted, I had another of those overwhelming urges to go up into the attic to find something. I looked in a dusty corner, near piles of wicker and daub cones for collecting swarms of bees. And there it was: another letter to her father in the First World War. On the back, he had written out the Morse Code in pencil. Why were these letters appearing in such extraordinary places?

Next day, Monday, I was painting clear varnish on to the red bricks and iron fireback in the yellow bedroom fireplace. Marguerite called to me very urgently. I was peeved. I was busy. I didn't want to stop varnishing and go up into the attic. The bristles of the brush would go hard if I left it. She wouldn't take "no" for an answer. With very bad grace, I stopped what I was doing, put on my gloves and overalls and climbed the stairs. She played "hot and cold" with me like a child in a treasure hunt. It was spooky. The "hottest" place was by the straw where I had already looked several times in the past. I knew there was nothing else there and told her so. It was not very clean and I didn't want to delve about in it. She insisted. I sifted through handfuls of the stuff, half believing I was crazy, half convinced I would find something. I did. I discovered another letter from the First World War. A long one. Paper had obviously been short and her father had replied on the blank part of the folded sheet. He was arranging some leave. It was absolutely fascinating.

I went to show Jack. I was on my way back upstairs when Marguerite was just as insistent that I should go into the salon. I tried to resist. I really did not like the room. It was still very dirty and although I had cleaned some of it up the previous September, it made my flesh creep. It was full of cardboard boxes of tools and things we had brought from England and I couldn't be bothered to start moving them.

Eventually I capitulated. Marguerite was like that. The thoughts she put in my head came out in English but they were often more like impulses than sentences. I had no idea what she wanted me to do. I went and stood by the open window and glanced sideways. There was some writing on the plaster but it had deteriorated too much to read easily. My interest caught, I looked more closely at the wall beside the window and was dumb-struck. There written in large uncoordinated letters at the eye-height of a small child was the word "MARGUERITE". The letters grew smaller as the writer reached the wall and did not have enough room for the original spacing. A foot above them, in basic primary school writing it said "Marguerite Xavier", and above that, in even neater writing "Marguerite Xavier" again. My heart racing as I drank in what felt to be a direct communication with her childhood, I turned to the next wall, where, even higher and in beautifully neat adult writing I saw: "Mademoiselle Marguerite Xavier, St Paradis, Limousin, France". Really fired up now, I went into the kitchen to get a torch. There was writing everywhere: inside the cupboard doors, on the back of the door, on two other walls. I couldn't see anything on the fireplace wall. Marguerite was determined that I should look under where some curtain poles leant against this blank wall. I was reluctant. It would mean climbing over four brimming cardboard boxes and anyone could see, even with a torch, that there was nothing on that wall. She was very impatient: "Go and look!" she shouted into my brain. I clambered over the boxes and moved the curtain poles, ready to reply crossly: "I told you so!" It was then I learned not to answer back. Under the poles I uncovered where Alain had written his name in pencil.

It was one of the most moving moments I can ever remember.

Analysing it, I concluded that the salon could not have been used as such for at least 90 years. Say that Marguerite was five when she wrote her name for the first time by the window. That would have been about 1905. Her parents would not have allowed a well-brought-up child to disfigure their dining room, so it had obviously not been in use at the time. She had also felt happy about adding her autographs on the subsequent occasions, which appeared to be years apart. The Vichy water bottles in the disintegrating crate dated back to this period, too. The room was an enigma. Had it ever been used for the purpose for which it had apparently been built? The plaster was bare and falling off in many places. The windowsill was non-existent and consisted of pieces of flat stone perched on top of the granite wall. A doorway through to the barn had been filled up with stone and mortar but the shape was clearly visible and it had been left unplastered. Another doorway which would have led to the back door before the stairs were built had been converted into a cupboard, whose doors were gaping and falling off. There was no sign of a fire ever having been lit in the grate — no blackening of the bricks or fire-back. There was, however, lots of evidence of workshop use. There were plenty of pencilled diagrams of woodwork and chalked sets of figures which seemed to show where people had jotted down measurements before they made something. Madame along the road had told us that she had taken cheeses down the cellar as a child in the 1920s to '30s (she was some 20 years younger than Marguerite) and had been afraid. She was unlikely to have done that in someone's best dining room. I also had the label from 1923 which had been found in the wood pile.

I dashed out to show Jack. He was busy and it was some time before he could accompany me to look at the writing on the walls. I could hardly find it. I discovered subsequently that the only time of day it could be seen without a torch, when the sun was in a certain quarter, was when Marguerite had commanded me to look. From that day onwards, neither of us questioned that she really was communicating with me. As a totally un-psychic person, I took it as a great compliment.

When Georges came to call at about 6pm we told him he could have the hay after all. He was delighted. We suggested that if he looked after the field he could have as many cuts as he liked. He was puzzled. We explained that in England, farmers got two cuts of hay a year. He said in the Limousin they managed only one. We were amazed that he could be bothered to tend our field for such a meagre reward, but he seemed very happy about the prospect.

We piled into his battered car and went round to the large barn where he kept his baler. When we inspected it we found that it wasn't English, it was Irish. He obviously didn't appreciate the difference. The plastic cogs in the bale wrapping mechanism were broken and he had been quoted about £1,000 for a new part by his dealer. He wondered if we could order a replacement from the manufacturers and also change the specification so he could wrap bigger bales. We noted down every word and reference number written on the machine and promised to do our best.

To thank us, he took us home for a little drink.

Georges was proud of his house, which he was renovating. He

showed us round, as one DIY enthusiast to another. We decided that his wallpapering was the most singular we had ever seen, especially on the stairs, where it started in triangles across the treads and finished in matching triangles across the ceiling.

We sat down at his kitchen table and he poured me a big glass of whisky and Jack a tumblerful of Ricard, telling him that it was traditional in the Limousin that you drank Ricard until you fell over. As we hadn't had any tea and Jack is more susceptible to alcohol than me (a hardened journalist) that was a good prophecy.

We really enjoyed Georges' company. We talked for a long time about all sorts of things, including councils, and enjoyed ourselves enormously. He was a good raconteur and we could understand him perfectly. The whisky and Ricard kept being topped up.

Then the room shook with an appalling noise. It was Georges' fridge-freezer which had erupted a few feet away. "That bloody thing," he said. "I've hit it with a spanner so many times and it doesn't do any good. My girlfriend and I haven't had a full night's sleep for months."

Though Jack was almost comatose, his practical instincts struggled to the fore. Either the motor or the heat exchanger was out of alignment and knocking against the casing of the appliance, he reasoned. He dragged himself over to the fridge-freezer and manipulated round the back. It was the heat exchanger. He adjusted the anti-vibration mounts and silence reigned.

Georges was beside himself. "If it doesn't wake us up tonight I'll buy you a bottle of champagne," he promised.

We chatted a bit longer and then he agreed to take us home. On the way past his vegetable garden he pulled up a fresh lettuce and filled a bag with brand new potatoes. We had them for tea and they were like ambrosia.

Jack had to go to bed early. For the first time in his life he was paralytic but at least he felt like a true native of the Limousin.

We spent most of the next day feeding wires down conduits running in vast spiders' webs around the gaps between the attic floor and the false ceiling. There are better ways of spending the time but not if you want to have lights in your house.

We gave ourselves a couple of hours' break during the afternoon. I had been having messages from Marguerite that we should have a look in the ash below the bread oven. But more practically, we were worried that burning the green wood during our New Year visit had added too much carbon to the chimney. We didn't want a chimney fire.

Jack found what we could only describe as an ancient 'scraper' in the dining room. It was like a spade with a short fat blade. He started to scrape all the deposited carbon out of the chimney with it, standing upright in the massive *cantou*, where he could see daylight out of the chimney above. The carbon pattered down and we filled four cardboard boxes with black chippings. We asked Paul if they could be recycled in the garden but he told us just to throw them away.

When we had scraped away all the solidified carbon we could reach, we set about the ash. There was a special compartment under the bread oven, on the left-hand side, which we had ignored for months. We had just stored kindling and newspapers in it. Marguerite had told me to look in there for something interesting and I wondered if it might be a crock of gold. The French of her generation notoriously mistrusted banks and the family had obviously been quite well-heeled.

Jack got a shovel and tried to empty the compartment. We filled four plastic dustbin sacks with powdered ash, sifting it all before we discarded it. We found fragments of newspapers, a recruiting poster for the Army and a number of intact half eggshells. There was nothing later than 1935.

We were disappointed not to have made our fortunes but gave up when we ran out of black plastic sacks. There was still a good nine inches of ash to go. We promised Marguerite that we would investigate next time we came to stay and we concluded that the last time bread had been baked in the oven was 1935.

At 6.30pm we heard a knock. It was Georges and his girlfriend, champagne bottle and new potatoes in hand.

"We slept undisturbed last night for the first time for months," he said. "I promised you a bottle of champagne and here it is!"

We invited them in, offered them a tin of fancy chocolate biscuits and opened the champagne. The least we could do was share it with them. Paul wandered over and we gave him some too. He said Elisabeth was busy with her sister and brother-in-law, who had come to stay. After he'd had a chat and gone home for his tea we got out all our treasures and showed them to Georges and his partner.

They were fascinated. What was even better was that Georges read the letters aloud. Our knowledge of French was not good enough to guess what was written when there was only the vague faded outline of a word to go on. As a native speaker Georges could tell just what it was. We could now understand exactly what the letters said. The couple thought we should offer all our "finds" to the museum in the *départemental* capital. We didn't say that the treasures were far too precious ever to part with. Anyway, they belonged to St Paradis. They were part of its very fabric. They went out of the house over my dead body.

Next morning we went to the capital to open a new deposit account at the bank. While we were there we wandered round the shops and bought one of the books of old photographs we had seen at Jan and Beatrice's home. Like all French books, it was horrendously expensive — about £20 for a large paperback — but we reckoned it was worth it so that we could identify our heirlooms.

We got some more glue for the coving in the yellow bedroom.

We were looking for ceiling roses for the yellow room, too. I had bought some lamp shades in the B&Q sale in England which could be used for the two new lights in the room and a bedside lamp. They were modern, very pretty and matched the curtains and duvets. All we needed to install them were some plastic ceiling roses, which one would have thought were simple to buy. We had searched the city and the capital and had not found a single one. We could not believe that something so basic had vanished from the shelves of all the *bricolages* in our part of the Limousin.

At our last port of call we found no ceiling roses but we did stumble across a special offer on imitation hanging oil lamps with integral roses. We decided to cut our losses and buy two for the yellow bedroom. They were not as nice as the one in our bedroom but they were in keeping with the house. We shelled out £12 each on them and agreed to put the pretty lampshades somewhere else.

Then Marguerite laughed. She told me she had hated my 1990s lampshades. She more or less hinted that she'd been responsible for the vanishing ceiling roses. And when we put them up, the "oil lamps" looked superb. They hung from plaster mouldings where real oil lamps had once been suspended. She had been right all along.

The following day was Wednesday. In the morning we stuck the coving up in the yellow bedroom and I painted it white. It made all the difference, as we covered over the black shadows between the false ceiling and the walls. The room was looking better than I had ever dared to hope.

After lunch we set off for the village where Marguerite and Henri had spent their married life, returning to St Paradis for annual summer holidays. She had become so real to me that she was almost a travelling companion.

The village, St Julien, was about 25 miles away — an hour's drive for us on unfamiliar roads but probably half a day's journey by horse and cart in 1920 — the year of their wedding. How had the couple met? Had it been an arranged marriage between two farming dynasties?

We found the village and drove to its centre where there was a beautifully modernised old church, a big square and a war memorial. I looked at the memorial. On three sides it bore the long sad toll of deaths in the First World War. On the fourth side, two additional names were immortalised: a man who had been killed in Algeria and Alain, the only person from the village to die as a result of the Second World War.

I can be quite pushy as a journalist but as me I'm very shy. I don't even like making telephone calls to friends. But Marguerite was beside me and I was full of courage. Old ladies peeped out at the foreign car behind their net curtains. I stopped the first person I saw in the street, an elderly man, and explained that we had bought Marguerite's family house in St Paradis. Did he know where she had lived with her husband in St Julien? She had been dead for 10 years, but he remembered her well. He directed us to their farm a mile away. It was set back from the road and looked busy and modern. We had no idea who lived there now and were too diffident to find out. I took some sneak photographs with a telephoto lens. It was enough to have tracked down Marguerite and Henri to their marital home and to know that Alain was immortalised on the memorial.

It was a beautiful day and extremely hot. On the way back we saw our first otter on the little lake between the town and St Paradis.

It was Thursday. When I woke I felt quite sick and had a stomach ache. I stayed in bed until 11am. When I decided to get up and open the shutters, Mme Vallet was passing. She asked if I was all right. She had seen the closed shutters and had been worried. She, too, had not been very well — perhaps there was a "bug" going round, she said. She invited us for a drink that evening.

While Jack toiled outside I pasted up the flowery patterned border under the new coving in the yellow bedroom. I had spent weeks in England finding exactly the right design to complement the duvet covers and curtains and was thrilled that it worked.

Still feeling fragile, I went to sit on the top of the granite steps from the back door into the garden. Jack had cleared a large area where the jungle had formerly reigned supreme and was flattening it out as he went along, redistributing the soil so that we could eventually have a terrace there. After enormous effort, he had dug up the stump and roots of a tree which Chris had chopped down the previous September. I had helped him to lever up a very large boulder near the window which ventilated the cellar. As I sat in the sun, idly gazing at the meadow, something caught my eye. I looked down and saw a brown and green snake slithering at speed across the newly dug area and into the undergrowth at the edge of the field. It all happened in a second or two.

Paul asked us over to meet Elisabeth's relations and to have a little smidgen of wine mid-morning. We told him about the snake and I described it. "A viper!" he exclaimed. "It's dangerous. You must be very careful!"

Word went round the village. The English had seen a viper! There was a tingle of shared excitement. The "Pinnies" remembered when, as children, they always had to wear boots and carry a stick before they ventured into the fields with the cattle, in case they encountered a viper. We had struck something deep in the folk memory. All our neighbours decided that Jack's gardening had disturbed the beast. We must be on our guard.

In the afternoon we went up to the cemetery to put the container of flowers on the Xavier family grave. It was possible to order miniature memorials to say who had provided floral tributes but we decided not to. Our flowers were for Marguerite as a tiny personal tribute, offered with our love, but we didn't want to offend any relations who might visit it. One thing really troubled me. The Marguerite who spoke to me was a woman of strong character: I felt I almost knew her. But I had no idea what she had looked like.

In the early evening we went to see the Vallets. We told them again how interested we were in the house and confided that the spirit of Marguerite was still there. They did not express any incredulity. We described what we had found and talked about Alain.

Michel said he and Alain had been the same age. They were close friends. Alain had been denounced to the Nazis: who knew why, perhaps for money? Michel said he himself had been just six days too young to be ordered to Germany for forced labour. He was eternally grateful for that.

Mme Vallet took up the wartime story. She told us how she had been stopped by a German patrol at the end of the day when she was returning home with her bicycle after tending the family cows. She came from a neighbouring village which was near the railway line — a target for saboteurs. There was a lot of Resistance activity in the area and many arms caches, which local people were aware of. She was too frightened to go straight home in case she was being followed and she wandered around for a long time before slipping back.

What about Henri? We knew so little about him except that he came from St Julien. He had been a *bon viveur* — Michel winked and raised an imaginary glass to his lips — but careful with his money.

I asked if Marguerite had been nice. Mme Vallet hesitated. "She was very religious," she replied. "And after her son died she was never the same again."

They showed us a lot of Vallet family photographs — the weddings of their children and Michel with his farm horses in the 1950s. He had loved them and never felt the same about the tractor which replaced them. We had to leave after about an hour because Jan and Beatrice were coming for supper. I was upstairs drying my hair when Jack called me. Michel was at the front door with an envelope.

"I have just found this for you," he said. "You are very welcome to borrow it if you wish."

He handed us a sepia photograph of Marguerite and Henri on their wedding day. It showed a pretty round-faced woman in her best clothes leaning on the shoulder of a handsome young man with a magnificent black moustache. It had been taken in a photographer's studio in the city. Marguerite looked like a cat who had got the cream. She obviously loved Henri to distraction and wanted to eat him up.

We were overwhelmed. We said we would take the picture to England, have it copied and bring it right back next time we came. Michel was happy and left it with us.

Once again, we felt the hand of Marguerite intervening. How many people could give you a copy of their best friend's parents' wedding photograph, in pristine condition, 75 years after it had been taken? Michel and Alain were not even related, so far as we knew. It was very bizarre — but we were ecstatic. Now we could put a face to the voice.

Friday was our last full day. Jack treated himself to doing something he had longed to do for months. He had brought a pump from England and was going to empty the well, in order to see how deep it was and how quickly it would fill up again. Paul and Michel joined in with gusto and helped Jack to remove the rotting sleepers which acted as a cover to prevent people and animals falling in. They prodded a long branch down the well and discovered that it was at least six metres deep.

After a lot of messing about, they got the pump going. I had been called in to video the phenomenon but had become bored when nothing happened. I told Jack I was putting the camera down on a stone by the chestnut tree. Jack did not hear me. Paul, playing with the hosepipe while the well emptied, sprayed gallons of its contents on top of the camera. Jack had to dismantle it, dry it and hang it out on the washing line. In spite of my protestations of innocence, I was not very popular and poor Paul was mortified — though it wasn't his fault.

By the evening it was working again, even if there were some funny lines on the picture for a day or two. I used it to immortalise the now finished yellow bedroom and all our other work. Paul and Elisabeth came over with her sister and brother-in-law for a last-evening social get-together and Paul brought us a bottle of extremely expensive Premier Grand Cru wine as a peace offering. I felt terribly guilty and stressed that the camera was perfectly all right.

He told us he was due to have another operation in September, when the cataract in his other eye would be removed. He had sailed through the procedure to rectify his detached retina and had no qualms about a mere cataract operation. Elisabeth was quite relaxed about it too.

We spent a convivial multi-lingual evening. Elisabeth could speak Dutch, French and English. Her sister and brother-in-law could speak Dutch, English and Spanish. We were OK in English and French but lost in Dutch and Spanish (which seemed to surface when someone couldn't think of an English word). Paul sat there, glass of red wine in hand, lost in a world of his own, thinking in French.

As we left next morning, I kissed him and he assured me: "Don't worry your heads about the Fat One. I'll tell her about the field."

We managed to get out of the village before her familiar tractor chugged into view.

Chapter Eleven

At home in Cheshire, Dave, the freelance photographer who took pictures for my paper was enthusiastic about copying Marguerite and Henri's wedding photograph. It was not often that he got his hands on a French studio portrait of that quality. He did the job very quickly and when I opened the envelope I discovered that he had made us two enlargements because he had been experimenting with concealing a slight blemish that neither Jack nor I had noticed previously. At least that was his story: I knew he was really just being kind and giving me two pictures for the price of one. I bought two gold frames and two sets of mounts. Now Marguerite and Henri look down on us from our dining room windowsill in Cheshire as well as taking their rightful place back at St Paradis alongside a montage picture of the three photographs from the family tomb.

They are posed by an intricately carved wooden chair with a high back and upholstered seat. The background is dark and shows a panelled wall and two long windows covered with curtains. It is impossible to tell if these are real or a painted backdrop. There is something two-dimensional about them. Henri wears a smart black suit, matching waistcoat, a high-collared white shirt with a stiff collar and a windsor knotted tie, and has a decorative watch-chain dangling on his chest. His black shoes are brightly polished and he is holding a document of some sort, rather uncomfortably, with one hand on the back of the chair. Marguerite is behind the chair, her hands cupped on his left shoulder. She is wearing polished boots and an expensive looking calf-length dress in a shiny material, with wide elbow-length sleeves. Sadly, the skirt is in shadow and only shows up where the light strikes the folds. Her hair is carefully waved and appears to have been arranged in a bun at the back, though that can't be seen. She has a pretty bracelet on her wrist and is nonchalantly showing a big ring on the third finger of her left hand. They are both gazing at the camera. Henri's dark hair is neatly combed and parted and his moustache is waxed and twirled upwards. He looks almost exactly

France was sweltering in a heatwave and the house was cool.

the same in the photograph which is on his memorial except that in the recent picture he is more relaxed and twinkly. He is a handsome man with attractive eyes. Marguerite is looking at the photographer with a completely open face. She is composed, happy and eager for the future. Henri, in his late twenties, looks like a man aware of his responsibilities as a newly married husband. He is stiff, proud and holding himself formally. Marguerite, younger than him, is uninhibited. Her hands on his shoulders say: "You belong to me at last." She is even standing so that the toes of their left feet are touching. The fact that she is crazy about him shines out of the picture after 70 years. It is a real honeymoon photograph.

The Fat One wrote to us almost immediately, asking if Paul was telling the truth about the field. Our hearts sank, wondering if she would threaten to sue us. We wrote a grovelling letter back, stressing how stupid we were and how we had discovered that Georges had been promised the land all along. We did not get a reply but imagined the political repercussions in the hamlet. We hoped it would all have blown over by the time we returned.

Jack had complicated correspondence and telephone calls with the manufacturers of Georges' silage baler in Ireland. He gave them all the details we had copied down from the various plaques screwed to the equipment but none of it meant anything. A new part like the one he wanted would cost about £700 plus VAT but there was no guarantee that it would fit his model. We visited the local agents who were equally vague. Eventually we discovered that it was one of three or four prototypes. We wrote to Georges explaining the situation and asking what he wanted us to do next. Paying the VAT alone on something ordered in England and going from Ireland to France posed a major problem in itself. How could Georges reclaim it?

We bought ourselves a secondhand trailer so that we could take bulky items over to St Paradis without having to hire a van. It had not been used for five years and needed a complete overhaul. Jack bought some new wheels and tyres and painted it a smart combination of British Racing Green and gold. I had just got a new company Nissan Primera and we had a towing bracket installed. Jack was busy in the evenings making things for St Paradis using his woodworking tools and I filled cardboard lettuce boxes with all sorts of bargains. Things were going really well, except at work for me, where they were pretty awful. The prospect of St Paradis kept me sane.

I am hardly ever ill or injured but it seems that Fate periodically asks us to pay for our pleasures at St Paradis by inflicting something nasty on me. A week before we left for St Paradis in mid September, during the 1995 heatwave, we took our dogs as usual for a walk round a couple of big fields which have been reclaimed from a chemical waste tip, using dredged silt from a local lake. It's a doggy paradise. We stopped to talk to another dog owner and were "buzzed" by little black flies which fed eagerly on me. Chris and I are always targets for insect life: they don't bite Jack and Alex. I didn't think twice about it.

For the next few days I had an irritating bite on my left hand, which I scratched and then ignored. From time to time I put some soothing cream on it. While we were on the ferry overnight it drove me mad and kept me awake in my bunk. Next day it was swollen and sore, so I bought some calamine lotion at our regular stop at Orléans and rubbed it on. For the rest of the journey my hand was covered in a pink cracking "shell" of calamine which disguised the fact that it was going a very funny colour underneath and getting bigger and bigger.

In an M6 traffic jam on the way down to Portsmouth Jack had said he had a present for me. He had handed me what looked like a pocket calculator in a leather case. It was an Ericsson mobile telephone. Chris and Linda both work for Ericsson as electronic engineers so it would have been more than our lives were worth to have bought another brand. He wanted me to have it for when I worked weekly late nights at the production department, and also because for some time we had worried about getting in touch with Jack's mother while we were in France. During the June holiday we had been faced with a canine crisis at home and malfunctioning local telephone kiosks. Jack decided to solve the problem with a GSM phone. We had thought of having a telephone installed at the house but France Telecom had not responded to our letters of enquiry about rates and installation charges.

All the way down through France we monitored the strength of the signal. It worked for 360 miles then went dead within a seven-mile radius of St Paradis. There were so few people around there that it was not commercially worthwhile to have a transmitter. Well — at least we could talk to Granny on the inward and outward journeys!

We had a very rough Channel crossing and when we arrived in France we saw debris blown all over the roads by gale-force winds which had wrought havoc in the north. When we arrived at the house the neighbours came out in force to make sure that we were all right. They had been watching the news and weather forecasts on the television and had been really worried about us. It was lovely to be the objects of such genuine concern.

When we looked around we could see that Paul and Georges had been incredibly busy. Georges had cut the hedge bordering the field — for the first time for years. It was a pretty drastic mechanical cut, with more gaps than hedge in places, but it was a great improvement. He had also cleared the undergrowth and brambles around the edges of the field and started to excavate a little stream for us where the water naturally drained down to a tiny waterfall in wet weather. We had talked to him in the past about our plans for a landscaped stream and had asked if one day in the future he could excavate the old pond with his digging machinery. We were glad we had brought him a large bottle of Jameson's Irish whiskey because the hay he would eventually get off the land would hardly recompense him for his labour.

Paul had continued to clear the back of the house: where there was now bare earth there had been a jungle 12 months before. He must have toiled for hours in the hot sun. We always brought him and Elisabeth presents — in spite of their protestations — and we felt that he certainly deserved his litre of best brandy this time, as always.

I washed my hands before we went over to see them and was horrified to see what a state the left one was in once the calamine lotion had dissolved. As soon as she saw it Elisabeth said I must go to the pharmacist the next morning to get some medication.

We got up early the following day, Saturday, to visit the pharmacy in the town. French pharmacists offer an invaluable service for minor health problems, we gathered. Except that he too, took one look at my hand and said I must go to the doctor's surgery. Our E111 would cover it. He told us the name of the road and we drove down there slowly. We saw a polished brass plate bearing a doctor's name screwed beside the door of a large house fronting on to the pavement. I pressed the bell and a distinguished woman in her late 60s answered it. I asked if the doctor was available. She looked distressed and said "My husband the doctor has died!" I was horrified. From her upset face it was probable that he had died very recently. I clasped her hand, apologising profusely and genuinely. She accepted my apology graciously and directed us farther down the street.

Half a mile along the road we found a large modern bungalow with a big sign saying "Surgery". From the names painted underneath we could see it was run by two married couples who were all doctors. We pulled into the car park and walked in cautiously. We were loitering by the reception desk, uncertain what to do, when a very good looking young man came out and asked if he could help. I said I had a problem with my hand and would it be possible to see a doctor without an appointment? I was English and it might all be a bit complicated.

He was charming. He replied that he had seen immediately that I had a bad hand and that if I waited he would see me presently. It didn't matter that I hadn't got an appointment and it certainly didn't matter that I wasn't French. He was sorry the receptionist wasn't there on a Saturday — he and his partner dealt directly with their patients on that day.

We sat in the waiting room on plastic chairs and made polite conversation with the others. In France you can't sneak in somewhere and bury yourself in a magazine. You are duty bound to say "*bonjour*" to everyone in sight or they will be very offended. The same applies to queues in bread shops and other similar situations. France is a very polite country.

After a quarter of an hour the doctor came to fetch me and conducted me to his consulting room. Jack came too. It was not one of your perfunctory "in and out" English consultations. He lay me down on his couch, examined my hand minutely under a special lamp, and checked all sorts of other things including my blood pressure. He said it was very high — perhaps it was the stress. I replied that I suffered from high blood pressure anyway but that it was rather difficult being ill in a foreign language. Shamelessly flattering (or perhaps to stop me self-destructing from hypertension) he told me I spoke French beautifully. I would have thrown myself under a train for him.

We had a social chat. I said I'd had mastitis at the New Year but had imagined there were no doctors on duty for something so comparatively trivial. He assured me that there was someone on call 24 hours a day and that if we ever had another problem we were not to hesitate about coming for treatment. He announced that the insect bite had become infected and gave me a prescription for cortisone cream and antibiotic tablets, then got out his metal cash box and said: "That'll be 110FF please!" There was none of this "Have a little word with my secretary on the way out" stuff. I felt he had earned twice that much. It would almost be worth being ill again, to be so cosseted.

We went back to the pharmacy to get the medicine. It was half as expensive as an NHS prescription. I rubbed on the cortisone cream immediately and my hand went bright yellow and became even bigger. It was like a grotesque balloon. Soon I could not move my fingers at all. Six months later I found out from a completely unconnected allergy test that I was sensitive to cortisone. Thanks to the antibiotics, but not unfortunately to the cortisone which I kept dutifully applying, my hand eventually got better after about a week.

Once again, like in January, I felt that I was not pulling my weight. At least it was not the right hand this time, I could write and cook though I couldn't hold anything in my swollen fingers. I watched Jack assemble a pine chest of drawers for the yellow bedroom — which still looked fantastic — and put up some shelves and a cupboard in the loo. He had made them in advance at home, as he had a clever window-frame contraption to go in the little window on the landing. When we bought the house it had a broken piece of gauze there, which allowed the building to breathe in the summer but let in icy draughts during the winter. Jack had made a frame with St Paradis oak which held a hinged gauze window and a piece of perspex which would take in and out and was secured by swivel catches. It was a very fine piece of work and Paul was full of admiration.

It was too hot to work outside. France was sweltering in a heatwave too, so we explored the field and surrounding paths, keeping in the shade. We noticed a number of cowpats: had the Fat One's cattle used the field anyway?

When we were back in the house Paul came over with a companion. We had told him the previous night about our experience with the GSM phone and how we would like a France Telecom one. Paul knows absolutely everyone and everyone knows him. Naturally he knew a man from France Telecom, who just happened to be passing. Whether Paul had phoned him in advance or had leapt out in front of his approaching van we never found out, but he had brought him over. The telephone man eyed up the site. No problem, he said. He wasn't busy next Tuesday, he'd come back and do the job then if we didn't want anything fancy. We gave him our details and he drove away. It was incredible. How unlike British Telecom...

In St Paradis it is impossible to have a gathering of two or three people in the middle of the road. Such an event acts as a magnet to everyone else. Soon all our friends were there swopping telephone advice, including Mme Vallet who had come along with a big bowl of Mirabelle plums specially for us. We felt glad to be home.

Next morning Jack went down the field to plant four oak saplings which we had been nurturing. He dug holes in the rock-hard ground along the inside of the hedge where Georges had cleared it. We wanted to mask an electricity sub-station which we could see from the house. When he had set the trees in the holes, Jack tied them to stakes and we made wire netting cages to go round them to protect them from rabbits. Operating a two-man bucket chain we watered them from the nearby public pond where some of Mme Echelle's ducks held court among the frogs.

It rained on and off, so we decided to go indoors and hang up some more pictures in the yellow bedroom. We already had a big floral watercolour that I had bought in June. In England I had framed four watercolour prints from a French calendar and we also had Marguerite's wedding photograph, which we put over the fireplace. The hearth was filled with a big vase of flowers and the effect was beautiful. We hoped she was pleased.

At lunchtime we were delighted to say a quick "hello" to Jan and Beatrice and we set a date later in the week for them to come round for supper.

In the afternoon we were waiting for a flying visit from some English friends who were en route to a cycling holiday in another part of the Limousin. We had promised them a conducted tour of the house. While we waited, Jack decided to go and make a cover for the well. We had brought the wood from England in the trailer and had a design in mind.

We removed the sleepers from the top and immediately found a snake floating on the water. It didn't move when we poked it and we hooked it out with a long stick. It seemed pretty dead but we consulted Michel and Paul about it.

"It's only a grass snake," they said. "They aren't dangerous."

To me it looked just like the snake which I had seen in June: perhaps it hadn't been a viper after all?

"No, no," said Paul. "What you described was certainly a viper. I have been looking out for it all summer."

I got a strong feeling that a good story would be spoiled if I hadn't seen a viper. I swallowed my misgivings. A viper it remained.

Michel and Paul wandered off and we saw another villager wending his way down the road, not in a straight line. He stopped, to be sociable. It was soon very obvious from his speech and the overpowering smell of stale wine that he was extremely drunk. Really out of his skull. I had never seen anyone quite so inebriated. He also wanted to help build the cover for the well and he was not going to take a polite "no" for an answer.

I felt very threatened and kept disappearing inside to get away from him. Jack was equally uneasy because there was no communication at all between the two men and he kept dragging me out to act as reinforcements.

The traditional design suggested by the villager was very sensible and we were grateful: we had been going to build the cover quite a different way and it would not have been so effective. However, his efforts at constructing it were horrifying Jack, "who is a measure it, glue it, screw it" kind of woodworker. The villager was a "hold it at arm's length, wave it about, threaten it with a six-inch nail and smash it (and your thumb) with a hammer" kind of woodworker. He was never able to co-ordinate the wood, nail and hammer: what can only be described as an abortionate Thing grew up under his hands, sprouting bent six-inch nails and without a parallel line or a right angle to its name. Jack had brought a strictly rationed amount of wood from England and he could see it all being eaten up by this one project. He was terrified that the neighbour would decide to use the powerful circular saw in the barn and chop a limb off. He was also afraid that the villagers would think the Thing was his handiwork and that he would lose his reputation for craftsmanship in one fell swoop.

Paul came across several times, saw what was happening, shook his head and silently went home again. Our friends from Cheshire saved the day. They arrived just as Jack was beginning to despair and we eventually made our co-worker understand that we had to stop because we had guests who had come all the way from England just to have a cup of tea with us. We thanked him profusely and he staggered off.

Next day, Jack could bear it no longer. Making sure there was no sign of the inebriated villager, he dismantled the Thing and made it again from scratch — with rebated joints, glue and screws. It stopped being a dog's breakfast and became an ordinary well cover which we covered with layers of wire netting to prevent leaves getting through and creosoted to protect from the weather.

It is now a Thing of Beauty.

We wonder if the villager gives himself credit for it when he sees it and mutters: "I don't remember making it as well as that!"

After our English friends had left, we had some supper and were sitting down in front of a cheerful log fire when we heard hooves outside. In a letter to my mother I described what happened next:

"We had a totally surreal experience... We looked up and saw a brown bull with about seven cows and seven calves trotting purposefully and completely unsupervised down the road. They immediately turned into our side entrance and gambolled off down the field! At the bottom they milled about for a time before one of them broke through the newly-cut hedge and they all climbed into the next field, which is otherwise inaccessible.

"We felt as though we were watching a nature programme on TV, when you see elephants or herds of wildebeest following the migration routes which have been set for centuries!

"The only snag is that we don't know when they will all decide to go home again and we don't fancy wandering down the field to be confronted by a bull and his family. We suppose it must be a fairly regular occurrence because the farmer hasn't been to find out where his animals are. Earlier today we planted four young oak saplings down the bottom of the field and we will be very cross if the cattle eat them."

We didn't know that this was just the beginning.

The wedding photograph stood on the mantelpiece.

Chapter Twelve

e were doing very well for homegrown vegetables. In addition to Mme Vallet's Mirabelles, we had received a bucket of *haricots verts* (which you eat whole) from Anne-Marie in return for lending her some of our decorating materials, and new potatoes, enormous tomatoes and *haricots secs* (which you take out of the pods) from Paul.

We went to the town in the morning then spent the afternoon busy with the house electrics. While we were up in the attic with our large halogen lamp for illuminating the wiring, we shone it all around to see if we could find any more things: Marguerite was keeping disappointingly quiet. We found a painted wooden sign measuring about 7ins x 9ins reading *"MAISON A LOUER"* ("house for rent"), which reminded us that someone had once said the house had been let for a short time, an old catechism in poor condition with "s's" like "f's" again and a very strange object which looked like a piece of wood padded with newspaper, covered with pink gingham and held together with big childish stitches that my granny used to call "homeward bounders."

Georges dropped by. We gave him his whisky and thanked him for all his work. We discussed the state of the vine, which had now re-established itself after its drastic pruning a year before and also asked him to prune one of our biggest trees which was causing offence to another neighbour by dropping leaves all over his garage roof. He had asked us to cut it down and we had refused, shocked. Tree life comes cheap in France and our attachment to our trees is a source of quiet amusement to friends at St Paradis. Paul is always telling us to chop down our favourite sweet chestnut which we think is majestic and beautiful. He shakes his head, saying the tree is too close to the barn and no good will come of it...

We kept an eye out for the bull and his family. They had moved from the fallow field, across the road and into a meadow already occupied by a Charollais bull and his family belonging to the Fat One. The village had echoed to much bellowing and threatening before the brown bull proved his superiority over the white one and stayed put.

My hand was getting better so I started doing some jobs of my own. I painted undercoat on the bare door to the downstairs lavatory and touched up the brilliant white areas on the back kitchen wall which had inexplicably gone orange.

The house was now really looking like a house inside. We were not "camping" any more and the temptation just to leave it at that and loaf around enjoying ourselves was very great.

The kitchen now could rival those of many of our friends in St Paradis. In the IKEA summer sale in Warrington we had picked up a pine dining table to seat eight people which was exactly the same as the one at home. We had installed it in our dining room in Cheshire and brought the old one — scratched where Jack assembled his metal woodworking bench on it — to St Paradis. We had brought our eight white chairs from home and replaced them with eight identical new pine ones. With a French plastic tablecloth covering the scratches and a bowl of flowers in the centre, it all looked completely authentic at St Paradis. Once our neighbours saw the table — regardless of all the rest of the furnishings in the house — they said with relief, "Ah, you're properly furnished now."

Also in the kitchen we had a fridge-freezer, a microwave, a butane gas cooker, a large oak desk (which we couldn't get up the stairs), a leather settee, a wooden food safe which Jack had made for our cheese and eggs, a hanging *batterie de cuisine* (also made by Jack) from which we hung all our saucepans and cooking utensils, a working surface beside the cooker made from an old fish tank stand, a white tea trolley with Alex's hifi unit and our records and tapes, our original pine table now used for food preparation and standing in front of the window, the IKEA leather settee and the upholstered chair I had re-covered, and a wooden clothes horse where we hung the towels and tea towels. Behind the door we had screwed up a set of coat hooks, and on the walls hung pictures and the clock which Linda and Chris had given me for my birthday. There was also a portable gas heater. The *cantou* was equipped with logs on one side and a set of hefty fire irons on the other, and we kept our kindling and firelighters in a box nearby.

The back kitchen had two sets of wooden shelves holding our food in tins, packets and plastic containers, together with all the crockery and glasses. A third set of shelves carried boxes of tools. Because it was cool we kept our bottles in a big wine rack and the vegetables in a set of metal baskets. Also in there were the washing machine and spin drier, cleaning implements and paint. A vase of daffodils stood in the window, which was decorated with a blue Laura Ashley curtain and French white net curtains, and there was a white wool rug on the floor, which we had made by hand during our engagement nearly 30 years before.

The lavatory had a handmade set of cupboards and (a mistake) a pink fluffy mat which was constantly covered with muddy footprints.

Upstairs, our bedroom was furnished with a man's compactum where we hung our clothes, a Victorian chest of drawers which I had half-restored and which was a ghastly shade of primer yellow, a pine double bed with matching duvet and curtains, a Victorian bedside cabinet with a wooden table lamp, and several rugs which matched the turquoise and orange in the general colour scheme. A vase of flowers stood on each windowsill, the fireplace was filled with a flower arrangement and the walls were covered with Victorian paintings which we had inherited. In front of the fireplace was a portable gas fire and above it I hung a wooden framed mirror dating from the 1930s, which had belonged to Jack's mother. On the mantelpiece was a glass candleholder, a model Irish Setter and a champagne bottle filled with flowers — the one we had opened in September to celebrate our first meal in the house. An old computer on a metal stand stood against the wall, waiting until it could go into the red bedroom when that became a study. On the compactum was an enlarged photograph of two of our puppies at their most adorable stage of development. It always made us smile.

The yellow bedroom had a double pine bed and a single pine bed. The duvets were matching primary colours and they co-ordinated with the curtains and the rugs on the floor. There was a new pine chest of drawers covered with a white linen and lace cloth and topped with a mirror, and a framed composite picture of Henri, Jean and Marguerite's mother from the photos on the tomb. A pine bedside cabinet which Jack had made stood between the bed and the window. The walls were covered with modern pictures in clip frames and some dried flowers. In the hearth stood a large arrangement of silk flowers in colours which matched the duvets and curtains. On the mantelpiece were two pottery candlesticks which Jack's mother had given us, and the wedding photograph of Marguerite and Henri. A corn dolly hung above. The curtain rails were dark oak to match the oak exposed on the varnished battens. I was inordinately proud of it all because everything had worked beyond my wildest imaginings.

The landing was covered with dark brown carpet tiles to level the uneven floor and keep the dust down.

The "bathroom" was still in its original state. One of the biggest jobs was to replace the rotten wood in the non-loadbearing lintel above the window.

The red bedroom, destined one day to be the study, had had its red wallpaper stripped off, its cracks filled and a new light installed. It needed to have its pink distemper ceiling stabilised — a task I was putting off. In the meantime it held Jack's bargain woodworking bench and the floor was covered with tools.

Downstairs, the dining room was as uninviting as ever. We had decided that we would never obliterate the names we had found written on the walls. We would either cover the whole thing with plasterboard and leave them to be discovered again by posterity, or we would renew the existing plaster but preserve the writing under glass at the appropriate points. The room needed a lot of money spending on it. It would require a completely new floor, for a start. But we could live quite happily without it and it was at the bottom of our list of priorities. In the meantime we used it to store all our materials for renovating the rest of the house.

The cellar needed to be cleared out. It had a mass of rotten wood on the granite floor which was making it damp. One day we would remove the trapdoor in the dining room floor, put balustrades round the flight of stone steps and an ornamental door at the bottom and tell our grandchildren it was a dungeon...

We just hoped that Alain hadn't stored any grenades down there.

During the afternoon we cleared up round the side of the bread oven building. We had not been able to gain access to the front half of the building but we took down and repaired the shutters over what proved to be a broken window and discovered that it contained brushwood to a depth of several feet.

We found that there was a carpet of broken bottles under the vegetation which had grown up alongside the bread oven building. Many of the fragments of glass which I picked up looked very crude and old. Someone had once told us that the village drunks used to congregate there. They seemed to have had a penchant for red wine.

The Vallets came round for a drink that evening. We wanted to thank them for lending us the picture of Henri and Marguerite and also for all their hospitality over the past year. They were good, solid friends. Every time they saw us they gave us fresh hens' and ducks' eggs which were quite out of this world.

When we brought out the framed enlargement of the wedding photograph, Michel was delighted and they examined it closely. The larger version showed features which were hard to see on the dark sepia original. We said that it had pride of place in the bedroom which Marguerite seemed to like so much. They repeated that Henri had liked his money and when we joked about looking in the bread oven for a pot of gold they hinted that it might not be such a crazy idea.

We talked about the bread oven building and they said that the ovens were built first and then the buildings were constructed later, around them. The ovens were fired with brushwood, which was why we had such a large amount stored in the front of the building. Presumably it had been there since the 1930s.

We showed them the dining room and its names. Mme Vallet was amazed that it had a fireplace: she had never noticed it before but was sure the room had never been a real *salle à manger*. They had always known it with a connecting door to the barn (now walled up) and had thought of it as workshop. That would explain why Marguerite's mother hadn't minded her daughter scribbling on the walls. The history books say that houses in this part of the Limousin were improved and enlarged in the 1870s, which would fit in with our home's timescale — so perhaps the Xaviers at the time had the room plastered and the fireplace put in along with the ones in our bedroom and the yellow bedroom, and fitted with an elegant window to match the others, but their successors never needed it as living accommodation. Maybe they required the bedroom overhead and the cellar below, but not the room itself.

We told the Vallets about the bull and his family, and they explained that the cattle belonged to an old man in the *commune* who was too ill to look after them any longer. Georges nominally kept an eye on them but during the current drought they were roaming from field to field, where the landowners tolerated the trespass as a way of helping their old neighbour.

Shown the strange gingham object which we had just found, Mme Vallet suggested that it had been used to store detachable collars. There were some perished strips of elastic around it which could have held a collar in place. It looked like the sort of thing a little girl makes at school and we wondered if it had belonged to Marguerite.

We were conscious that Marguerite had asked us to dig out the ash container under the bread oven and had been cross when we left the job half-done in June. Next morning we cleared the decks, brought out some black plastic bags and a cardboard box and started to shovel. We went through each spade-load and found lots more egg-shells and pieces of newspaper but nothing significant. We were beginning to despair: what was she getting at? There were no coins in there, nothing of monetary value. But in almost the last shovelful we found a rectangular piece of glass. On close inspection it was a 19th century photographic plate with a portrait of a woman on it. How on earth had it found its way into an ash-container? We were afraid that if we cleaned it, we might remove the image as well. But we were delighted with our find.

We looked forward to the arrival of Paul's man from France Telecom. Indeed, we never left the house for days in the hope that he just might arrive. We learned that France Telecom can be just as slow and bureaucratic as all other nationalised concerns. Paul became very embarrassed, taking the man's non-arrival personally. The telephone lines were red-hot each day between his house and the local office where he was given empty promises to keep him quiet. During the afternoon of the day before we were due to leave, a France-Telecom van drove slowly down the road and I ran from the kitchen almost into the arms of the man driving it, saying: "It's us! It's our house where you're supposed to be installing the telephone!" He looked mildly surprised at being accosted by a mad Englishwoman in paint-splattered overalls and replied, looking at a computer print-out, that he had come to check the practicalities of our installation. Exasperated, I explained that this had already been done by a colleague who'd said: "No problem!" There was a metal bracket on the side of the house where our neighbour's wire was carried and a telegraph pole a few feet away in the other direction.

He agreed there was no problem. But his colleague had not filed the correct paperwork. Then I called Jack (and all the neighbours turned up for the entertainment value) and we started to discuss the details and what kind of telephone we would have — and where. We specified that we wanted the very cheapest handset, since it would only be used in emergencies. Both of us hated speaking French on the phone so there was little chance we would be ringing our compatriots up for long chats. Indeed, if anyone French rang us, we would probably have a collective heart attack. We just wanted to be available to our sons and elderly mothers in England.

He agreed that someone would come back the following Tuesday, after we had gone home, to install a line in the kitchen and an extension socket in the bedroom. We didn't really want the latter but Paul insisted — it was free if it was done at the time when the phone was put in. We would have plummeted in his estimation if we had not had something that was going free. Paul promised to let the engineer into the house and show him the spots on the walls where we wanted the sockets. It was only after the man had driven away that we realised Paul was going to have his cataract operation on the Tuesday. Elisabeth would have to do

155

the honours with the key — if she wasn't at the hospital with him. We decided that the telephone was doomed.

We had other things on our minds, however. The bull was back.

He and his family had stayed with the Fat One's Charollais cattle for two or three days after he had established his superiority in an initial shouting-match. We had checked on them every day before we ventured out.

Jack was spraying weedkiller on the old jungle site out the back and I was painting window-frames in the back kitchen after putting a top coat on the lavatory door and deciding that the old grey oak window frames looked very shabby. What paint they'd had on them had long ago peeled off. It was while I was applying primer to the back kitchen window that I saw the cattle leaving the Fat One's field. Jack saw them at the same time. We met at the top of the granite steps to the back door, where we could make a quick retreat if necessary. We were due to tidy ourselves up and go to the Vallets for an *aperitif* in about ten minutes.

That evening I wrote to my mother: *"We watched the brown bull's cows walking into our field by the main entrance. The bull was on the little communal path which runs along the left-hand side of our land, together with the calves. The bull made his majestic way into the field but the calves were frightened by a car and ran back down the path. Their mothers went to reassure them over the wall and some calves clambered over it to get into our field. The bull followed, ate one of our new oak trees and then pawed the ground and rolled beside another one! The rest of the calves came back through the original hole in the hedge. The bull is now ensconced outside the back door, chewing the cud and looking very satisfied. He is absolutely enormous and has a wound on his shoulder, presumably where he had the punch-up with the Charollais. The calves are standing round the remains of Jack's bonfire sniffing the smoke, while the cows are being All Girls Together down the field.*

"We talked to the Vallets about it again. They asked if we wanted Georges to come and take the cattle away but we thought that would really let the side down and said we were quite happy for them to be there. They must be hungry poor things, the drought has been awful and we've got some good grass. We don't mind helping the old man, like everyone

else. We very tentatively asked if the bull was dangerous: we stressed we
weren't timorous townies but that in England farmers used artificial
insemination and one didn't come across big bulls like that very often.
Michel said, No, no, they weren't dangerous — unless you met them in
the road. You would have laughed if you had seen us walking home down
the lane from their house. It's only 200 yards but we were working out
an escape plan just in case."

We joked about it when we had our usual farewell drinks with Paul and Elisabeth that night and we were relieved to know that we weren't the only people to be a bit uptight. Paul said that one of the "Pinnies", country born and bred, was terrified and would hardly venture out. She lives near the grass footpath and it certainly wouldn't be funny if she bumped into the bull on it.

When we got up in the morning to do our packing the cattle had gone and someone — it must have been Georges, at crack of dawn — had made us a crude gate out of stout tree branches which he had tied to the stone gateposts. It was more a gesture than a real deterrent but we were grateful that he had gone to the trouble. The real tragedy was the once-sturdy oak saplings, planted so carefully and so recently. They had been two or three feet high, protected by wire and stakes and sprouting lots of leaves. They had all been eaten to within about nine inches of the ground and one had been rolled on and its stake broken. We repaired them as best we could and hoped nature would take its course.

Marguerite had been very quiet on this trip after having felt like a constant companion during June. I was sad. Was she angry because we had told our friends about her? I apologised and said that I missed her.

It wasn't until I was doing the last-minute tidying that she came back. The only time the house at St Paradis looks neat and tidy is the moment that we shut the front door to come home. We clutter it with junk when we arrive and we spread all our tools about while we are there. Jack cannot see a flat surface without putting two power tools, a screwdriver and a box of electrical bits on it. Our dining table is eight feet long and we eat off the final two feet of it...

I was dusting in our bedroom. Dust and dirt permeate through the gaps in the floorboards of the attic above. The exposed beams and boards look beautiful but they are not very practical. The mantelpiece was very dusty. I had some furniture spray in my hand from cleaning the wardrobe and I sprayed a little on the top of the mantelpiece. I had not done this before in case we needed to strip down the wooden fire surround to revarnish it. I didn't want to add to the layers which needed to be removed, but something made me do it this time.

The small section I had polished gleamed. Indeed the champagne bottle with the flowers was reflected in it. Marguerite was back. "Do some more!" she commanded. I did the whole mantelpiece. It shone. "Do the sides!" she said. They shone. "Do it all again!" she said. I did — several times. She was really excited. Each application of the polish made an enormous difference. Where once the mahogany fire surround had just "been there", part of the room but not a feature, now it took a dominant place. It was extraordinary what some elbow grease and modern furniture polish would do.

"I want you to hang my picture over it!" she said. I remonstrated. The 1930s mirror was useful over the fireplace. We combed our hair in it when we got up. She was adamant. I put the mirror in the yellow bedroom over the fireplace and moved her wedding picture to the nail we had inherited over the fire in our bedroom. I didn't like it there but she was pleased. I pulled the portable gas fire to its place in front of the hearth and replaced the ornaments on the glowing mantelpiece.

"I've done that for you," I said. "What are you going to do for me?"

"You've found nearly everything now," she replied. "But I will show you something you have forgotten."

She led me to a cardboard box where I had put some of our original finds in September. Inside I discovered a beautiful board game, called "The Game of the Goose", played with counters and giving forfeits and rewards. She was right. I had found it on the first day in the red bedroom, mistakenly put it in the box of things which I had regarded as "worthy but boring" and not given it another thought for a year. It was a true "treasure".

She told me to open a little tin box which contained small items of haberdashery. Again, I hadn't found it very interesting. At the bottom I came across a tarnished brass button showing a hare in flight. "Keep that with you and remember me by it," said Marguerite.

I cleaned it up and we keep it safe in the leather handbag Jack uses in France.

We analysed why Marguerite might have stayed away. She could have been punishing us for talking about her, but it was more likely that she hadn't been interested in what we were doing. We had not wrought any great transformations on this trip, apart from the downstairs loo, which now looked great. We had been gardening and doing a lot of grovelling about, shoving wires down conduits. Judging by the appearance of the original electrics, Marguerite hadn't been much exercised by that either. It was when we decorated rooms or I did "housewifely" things that she appeared.

We were so pleased that she hadn't left us. A very sensible friend in England who knows about these things from personal experience said she thought Marguerite had "chosen" us as proper custodians of the house and would stay until she was satisfied that we had done a good job. We hoped we would live up to her expectations.

I clung to St Paradis as a lodestar in a turbulent world

Chapter Thirteen

I had thought I had to pay for the bliss of St Paradis with the nuisance and pain of my infected hand. How wrong I was! The price was much higher.

We arrived home in Cheshire at lunchtime on the Sunday. I went back to work the next morning. I had only been there about ten minutes — just long enough to start telling my colleagues about the bull — when there was a phone call for me. It was the secretary of one of the other editors. She said he was making the rounds of the branch offices that morning. I asked what this had to do with me — his paper was quite separate from mine. She was surprised. "Don't you know? He has just been made editorial director. You should have had a fax on Friday."

My heart sank. I had no respect for him and knew I could not work with him. It was mutual. On the Thursday morning, in the middle of a management course at head office on how to get the best out of your staff, I had to report to him to be told that the editorial department was being restructured and my job would be redundant. I had worked for the company for 15 years: four as a feature writer, one as a chief reporter and ten as founder editor of my paper. The past year had been purgatory as I felt I was forced to lower my standards and produce a publication that was so minimal that I was ashamed of it. The excuse was the soaring price of newsprint but I was sure the real reason was greed and shortsightedness. The company had been put up for sale and the bottom line was the only thing that mattered. The quality of the product was immaterial. It was hell-bent on killing the goose that laid the golden egg, but was too stupid to see that.

I drove home from head office in a daze; my eyes pricking with tears I was too proud to shed and my chin jutting out. "Bastards!" I kept repeating under my breath.

Jack had got the day off to take part in a traffic survey he organises for the village every two years. He had booked a microfilm reader at a reference library in Wales for the afternoon, to do some family history research. We went over together and spent three hours tracing ancestors. We counted ourselves lucky to track down their dates of birth, marriage and death, and this helped me to see my own life in perspective. They must have had crises and dramas, but no-one knew about them a hundred years later.

Behind the anger and resentment was a persistent voice in my head which kept telling me that this could be a new beginning. Why live in purgatory if you can escape? We had paid off our mortgage three months before; Chris had finished at university and we no longer had to support him. It was time for a change of direction.

I accepted the redundancy immediately. The money wasn't astronomical but it was better than nothing. We would be able to continue to eat for a while. There was vague talk about the possibility of something else but I wasn't interested in going through the motions. If the company didn't want me and thought so little of my efforts, then I certainly didn't want anything to do with them. I was going to walk out with my head held high, having made no compromises at all. I wasn't the only one: three other male colleagues at my level and higher had been given the same news. Sadly, their financial and family circumstances forced them to compete for the proffered "alternatives."

Statutory things were gone through. After the redundancy was confirmed I agreed to produce one more issue of the paper. I had been determined to be brave and dignified but when I put the phone down after the final call to the new editorial director, I turned to my colleagues and said: "Sorry folks, that's it. I'm going." And burst into floods of pent-up tears. I was glad to quit a company I had come to despise but devastated about leaving my staff and friends. I had always run the office as a family and to turn away from it was as big a wrench as abandoning my children.

People were wonderful. Everyone was outraged at the way the four editors had been treated and we had enormous support across the board. Our fate constituted a "saga" in the trade press for several weeks. I had four leaving parties and an avalanche of letters and cards. The decision came so suddenly, and I decided to go so quickly, that my colleagues in all departments reacted spontaneously. Some of the letters and messages I received were almost like love letters in their passion. It was good to know that if the management was careless of my skills and experience, they were appreciated where it mattered, amongst my peers. One particular old friend who is an editor in another part of the company, was a tower of strength and kept in constant touch. It was also nice to learn that the readers would miss me. I printed a piece in my last paper saying that I was "going to spend more time with my family" (which everyone knows means you've been kicked out!) and I received great support from the people for whom I had tried my best to provide a service for the past ten years. The chief executive of the borough council wrote me a letter which I treasure.

The day I left I brought home enough bouquets to decorate every room in the house. Jack came to my lunchtime farewell "do" in the local pub to give me some moral support and drive me away afterwards. I had insisted that my "do's" were positive: that I wanted to thank everyone for what we had achieved together and not be miserable. I demanded that they were celebrations. Nevertheless there was hardly a dry eye in the place when I finally said goodbye to my own office colleagues. I felt as though I was throwing them to the wolves.

However rational one tries to be about such a major event as redundancy, the body and emotions react in a way which is divorced from what the brain is telling them to do. I wanted to settle down, take stock of the situation and have a rest but instead I became hyperactive. I had the fortnightly ritual humiliation of signing on at the Job Centre and knowing there wasn't a single thing on the boards that I could do, or wanted to do. I had rejected newspaper journalism and inclined more and more to freelance writing and page design. I joined the Society of Freelance Editors and Proofreaders. I was shortlisted with two others for a sub-editing job in Liverpool which could have meant travelling the world.

But mostly I cleaned the house.

I was horrified how shabby it had become under the constant pressure of five dogs. I had also been too tired for a long time to summon up any enthusiasm for being houseproud. Now I was forced to become a housewife I decided I would be the best one in Christendom. I reckoned that if I could enjoy doing it in our house in France, which was twice the size of our semi in England, I could force myself to enjoy doing it here.

I clung to St Paradis as the lodestar in a turbulent world. To cheer ourselves up, we booked to go to St Paradis for the New Year again — but for longer this time. As soon as I lost my job I wrote to Elisabeth and Paul to tell them. Elisabeth had a close relation in Holland who worked as a magazine journalist for the same international company and could well have been facing the same fate. Elisabeth wrote back: it could be a blessing in disguise for me, she said. We would have so much more time to come to St Paradis. Work was not everything. I thought about how simply she and Paul lived, what problems they had overcome and how happy they were. She was right.

In early December I had a call from the borough council whose chief executive had been so kind. Would I like to go and work temporarily for about five months as their part-time press officer while the incumbent was on maternity leave? I agreed immediately. I liked the council and its officers, I knew the town and I knew the press — it was a tailormade job. I would start the day after we returned from France.

The spring returned to my step: someone wanted me after all.

Chapter Fourteen

Chris and Linda came to stay for Christmas. They had graduated with good marks in the summer, were engaged now and were working in West Sussex for Ericsson. Their wedding date was set for August 2, while Alex and Michelle had decided to tie the knot on August 31. We were all going to have a busy year in 1996...

Even in our temperate part of Cheshire there was a White Christmas and it was bitterly cold. "Weather" stories dominated the news on the television and radio. The whole of Europe shivered, including the Limousin.

On Thursday, December 28 Chris and Linda returned down South while Jack packed our car ready to set off for Portsmouth later in the day. We had handed back my new company car the morning before — three months after I was made redundant — having in November bought ourselves a second-hand Peugeot 405 diesel turbo estate on the grounds that it would be patriotic in our adopted country and ideal for travel in France.

As a "lady of leisure" I'd had time to plan the packing in advance for the first time and it was all parcelled up neatly in lettuce boxes from the local supermarkets. As well as the normal furniture, tools and necessities, we had as usual bought boxes of chocolates and biscuits as New Year presents for our friends, and we planned to buy bottles of duty-free whisky on the ferry for those who had been particularly helpful during the year.

A special project for me was to finish a fascinating 1040-page trilogy (translated into English) by the well-known French writer Claude Michelet which depicted a Limousin farming family saga over three generations from 1900 to the 1980s. I had stumbled across it in a magazine book review and ordered it immediately. Then before Christmas Jack's aunt in Lincolnshire quite independently recommended it to us as required reading and said she had been captivated by the story. I took it that Marguerite had a hand in all this somewhere. The books followed her life and experiences exactly. She was born in 1900 and died in 1985. The three

I had a sudden urge to paint the kitchen white.

books felt like a personal message from her and I savoured the prospect of reading them in the surroundings about which they were written.

In woolly hat, thick gloves and padded mountaineering anorak, Jack listened to the Peugeot's radio while he spent several hours packing the vehicle like an intricate 3-D jigsaw puzzle. All the doors were open while he stuffed in our luggage, tools and equipment for St Paradis. Everything fitted very satisfactorily. Occasionally we looked with academic interest at the thermometer on the outside wall: it read minus 10 degrees Centigrade.

At half-past four we locked the house, said goodbye to Jack's mother, jumped in the car and turned the key in the ignition. Nothing happened. We tried the things you do when your car won't start — to no avail. We decided that Jack had either drained the battery by listening to the radio and leaving the doors open (activating the interior lights), and/or that the diesel had frozen. Our magic departure time of five o'clock came and went. Instead of being relaxed and early we were going to be extremely frazzled and late. At 5.15pm we got a spark of life out of the Peugeot and roared off, nerves on edge. Our tempers weren't improved by interminable traffic jams on the M6 between Holmes Chapel and Birmingham. However at Portsmouth there were fewer passengers than usual on the ferry and we set sail dead on 10.30pm for probably the very first time.

We love going to France but we hate the bit between starting to pack the car and driving up the ramps on to the boat. As an experience it ranks with going to the dentist or finding a note from the boss on your desk saying "See me".

It was a rough passage but we disembarked at 7am and had our best journey to St Paradis arriving, after stops for breakfast and lunch, at 3pm. The volume of snow in the Limousin was just the same as it had been in Cheshire but it was melting rapidly. The digital thermometer in the kitchen registered 3.5 degrees Centigrade outside and 5.5 degrees inside. It felt quite tropical.

The best thing about our arrival was the fire. We found an enormous oak log blazing in the *cantou*. It took up most of the fireplace and judging from its size had been burning for a long time.

On the table we discovered a cardboard box containing our new telephone. It was much more sophisticated than we really needed, for we only wanted a phone in case of emergencies at home in England. We examined the walls: France Telecom had installed the connections in exactly the right places in the kitchen and our bedroom. Someone had obviously given them the right instructions even if Paul had been in hospital having his cataract removed. Elisabeth had already written to confirm that everything had gone very well with the operation.

We plugged the telephone into its socket, put it on top of the freezer for want of a better position — and forgot about it. While we were unpacking it rang.

We froze. We hate answering the telephone in French. Picking up the receiver is an action which guarantees that the French-functioning part of the brain will be wiped completely blank. Jack eventually answered it. It was Elisabeth. "We wanted to be your first callers," she said. "Will you come over for a drink?"

We were so relieved it was her that we needed the drink to steady our nerves.

We thanked Paul for the fire. He said that he and Maurice had found a fallen oak tree in the fields two days before and had dragged an enormous log back to the house. They had started a fire with it in the *cantou* and had been so captivated with the scene that they had sat on the leather settee in front of it for the rest of the afternoon enjoying the nostalgia of an open fire. Their houses were equipped with much more efficient — and soulless — wood-burning stoves but the blazing log took them back to their youth. It had been burning since Thursday.

After a couple of hours' chat we picked our way home through the snow to carry on with the unpacking. I dumped some towels and linen in our bedroom and went into the yellow bedroom to put a new white counterpane on the single bed. I stopped in mid-stride in the doorway. The floor in front of me was covered with a thousand shards of broken glass.

The 60-year-old rope had rotted on the wooden framed mirror which Marguerite had "asked" me to move from our bedroom into the spare room and it had fallen off the wall, shattering all over the rug and floorboards. On the way down it had knocked off a dried flower ornament on the mantelpiece, which was relatively undamaged. This had stood where Marguerite's wedding photograph had been placed until I got her urgent instructions to move it next door.

If I had left the mirror in its original place over the fireplace in our bedroom it would have smashed the glass treasures on the mantelpiece and fallen into the portable gas fire, causing much more damage and mess. It was all very strange. Had she known that the rope was at breaking-point and given me an oblique warning?

I cleaned the tiny mirror splinters up, but every time I went into the room over the next few days there would always be a shard somewhere, winking at me from a crack in the floorboards.

We "christened" the new telephone by ringing Alex and my mother. Chris reciprocated by calling us from Linda's parents' flat in Kent. It was all very civilised.

To celebrate the Christmas and New Year season we hung a holly wreath, which we had brought from England, on the salon's front door. It looked really festive and attractive against the blue-grey paint and put us in the mood for *le Nouvel An.*

The house was still only a few degrees above freezing and we felt the chill when we stopped bustling around. We lit the gas fires but they had an uphill struggle to make much impact on the cold stored in the granite walls during the Arctic temperatures of the previous weeks. The 15-tog duvet and the electric blanket made the bed welcoming but during the night the very thickness of the duvet stopped it nestling around our bodies and we slept fitfully, our shoulders cold where the icy air could creep into the gaps.

We had a lot to do the next morning and set the alarm for 7.30am. It was very hard to drag ourselves out of bed. The digital thermometer registered six degrees in the kitchen and outside, but we soon managed to raise it to 15.5 in the kitchen with two gas fires and the log fire. The big log had finally smouldered and gone out during the night and Jack was able to insert behind it a massive steel fireback which he'd made in England. We had decided that most of the heat from the fire went straight up the chimney and we needed a fireback to radiate it into the room. It worked very efficiently — the extra heat was palpable.

After breakfast we went into the town to hire two new gas bottles. As usual the people in our old-fashioned ironmongers couldn't find the right forms and didn't know how to fill them in when they eventually discovered them. We decided they could not have many new customers. We wanted to support local businesses but they didn't make it easy.

After lunch we drove to the *départemental* capital where we did the rounds of the DIY stores and spent a fortune on a fitting for the fusebox. Jack wanted to concentrate on rewiring during this trip, as outside jobs would be almost impossible.

Mme Vallet brought us the address of a furniture stripper in the nearest city, who could do a professional job cleaning off the appallingly filthy paint on the upstairs doors. I felt able to tackle most jobs but these doors turned my stomach. I could never work out why they had got into such a disgusting state when the ones downstairs were only shabby. Nothing else in the house was so unpleasant and all our evidence pointed to the Xavier family as being very respectable and clean.

As proud owners of a telephone we also had a phone book. In the usual French way it was catalogued by commune rather than in alphabetical order of surnames for the whole large area it covered — like an English telephone directory. I studied it closely. At last I knew the identities of some of our neighbours who had previously just been welcoming faces — and I knew how to spell the names of the ones we had never seen written down. The same surnames occurred again and again, through vast family networks. We even discovered Elisabeth's Dutch surname for the first time, as the phone was registered in her name. It had never occurred to us that we had known and loved her for well over a year without being aware of her full name.

That night we put a 4.5 tog duvet in a cover and popped it underneath the thick one. It settled itself comfortably into the curves of our bodies and we were warm enough at last. In the past the prospect of a quilt with a combined value of 20 togs had seemed unthinkable. Now it was a necessity.

When we woke up it was Sunday and New Year's Eve. Elisabeth had invited us over to a big party which was to be held in her house that night and we were looking forward to it after the fun we'd had the year before.

In a quiet moment, I went back into the dining room to see if I could find any more writing on the wall. I discovered some, but it was impossible to read. In a foreign language, you often can't guess the word from the overall shape of the letters, as you can in your own tongue. It is very frustrating. The plaster around the original writing was deteriorating and I was afraid that it would crumble away before we could immortalise the graffiti.

During the morning I persuaded Jack to take the old plastic seat off the lavatory and replace it with a wooden one we had bought months before. It was so cold that sitting on freezing plastic was enough to put us off answering the calls of nature. The wooden seat was more stable and much more user-friendly.

We hung a curtain behind the landing door to the attic, cutting out the icy draught which whistled down the stairs and into the kitchen, and I used my grandmother's old Singer sewing machine to hem the lined curtain we had hung across the front door during our visit in September. I had left it pinned, so that I could judge the required length when it had dropped over a period of time.

Each new insulation job made the house more bearable but we still each needed our St Paradis winter gear of thermal vest, long johns, lumberjack shirt, thick trousers, woollen socks, stout shoes and fisherman's jersey. We looked like tubby Michelin men, especially when I wore salopettes instead of trousers.

It was in this spirit that I approached dressing for Elisabeth's party. I knew in my heart that her tiny kitchen and dining area would be like an oven when they were packed with 18 people but I couldn't bring myself to strip down to just my best Viyella dress, normal underwear, petticoat and 15 denier tights. Leaving off the thermal vest and hiking socks seemed like tempting Fate to give me a dose of pneumonia.

So when the time came, we took over eight of our dining chairs and half a homemade Christmas cake (which was my contribution to the feast), plus our anoraks and a thick cardigan for me. Anne-Marie was already there, laying the tables which had been brought from Paul's bistro and placed end to end to fill the room. Busy in the kitchen were a sweet French couple from Paris, old friends of Paul and Elisabeth, who had brought their Dachshund with them. The wife was making wonderful things from simple ingredients and the husband was attacking oysters with a fearsome implement. As usual, I felt my culinary skills were quite inadequate.

We chatted and helped rather ineffectually. I was nearly passing out. There were only seven of us in the room but the stove had been stoked up and it was like the Arizona desert. Sweat dripping off my nose, I rolled my sleeve up to reveal the Arctic expedition quality thermal vest and told Elisabeth I would really have to go home to change before I expired of heat-stroke. They had also run out of glasses, so with the promise of lending them some of ours, Jack and I set off home.

Before we reached the back door there was a streak of lightning along the floor and an expletive from Jack. The Dachshund had got him by the leg. With great embarrassment its owners explained that it didn't mind people coming into a house after it had arrived but it didn't like them leaving... They held it down while we escaped. Later examination showed that its teeth had sunk through his thick corduroy trousers and his socks to remove the skin of his calf. Jack couldn't understand it — dogs usually adored him. He put a plaster on and resolved to be wary.

I stripped off several layers of clothes and we went back, clutching a box of wine glasses. The Dachshund was pleased to see us. Jack restrained himself from giving it a swift boot up the backside when no-one was looking.

A great influx of Dutch people then started to arrive. There are hardly any English in our part of the Limousin but it is popular with people from Holland who, while integrating well, also form a little community of their own. Each family had brought a lavish contribution to the evening meal in addition to the spread put on by Elisabeth and Anne-Marie.

Thirteen Dutch, two English and three French sat down at 9pm to welcome in the New Year. Jack and I sat with Elisabeth, Paul and the Parisians, who were hearteningly easy to understand and very good company.

We often despair that our grasp of French never seems to improve, but we forget that most of the time in our little corner of Deepest France we are battling against the equivalent of a Glaswegian accent before we even penetrate the French words. People who speak the sort of French you learned at school are a pleasure to converse with, often because you can mimic the grammatical structure of their speech patterns and appear much more fluent than you would have been if starting from scratch. That's impossible if someone is talking to you in dialect.

We ate and drank for six hours in a gloriously stretched-out banquet. We consumed a mountain of food and a couple of bottles of wine each (not to mention the champagne and liqueurs), but no-one got drunk or sick because it was all done a little at a time.

I counted thirteen courses at the time and made a list of the eleven that I could remember afterwards, just out of interest:

* Oysters
* Langoustines
* Fresh and smoked salmon
* Asparagus
* Roast beef and haricot beans
* Dutch pastries
* Petit fours
* Fruit salad with lychees and kiwi fruit
* Artichoke hearts with boiled eggs
* Avocado pears and terrine
* Crisps with guacamole

Our poor Christmas cake just didn't get a look in. No-one had room for it at all, so we took it home and ate it ourselves during the rest of the visit.

The Crazy Horse strip club was on the television again but Paul switched over to a programme of drunken community singing by a studio full of celebrities which would have been music to the ears of an anthropologist and certainly material for a thesis. The words of the songs were sub-titled on the bottom of the screen and everyone except Jack and I (who didn't know the tunes) joined in with gusto. Anne-Marie polka-ed round the tiny open spaces in the room with her Dutch friends, while the famous faces on the television blubbed and perspired, raised their glasses and sagged against each other, in a tuneless orgy of self-indulgence.

At midnight we all lined up to embrace everyone in turn and wish each person a happy New Year. I am not sure if the custom is Dutch or French, but it's delightful. Then the Dutch lit sparklers and went outside to have their traditional fireworks. They enjoyed themselves hugely, lighting bangers with total abandon on the back doorstep, within inches of their cars. Jack, schooled in the ICI regime of "avoiding unsafe acts" at all costs, was a nervous wreck and the Dachshund retired terrified to a shopping basket in the kitchen.

About 2am Elisabeth took the Dachshund on her knee and fondled it, while chatting to Jack. He thought he ought to make a gesture of reconciliation to the dog and stroked it on the head. It bit his hand.

At 3am people started to drift away and we made our excuses, too. It had been a marvellous evening. The Dutch had been welcoming and told us all about their experiences in the area. One of them was even a freelance page designer — which was what I had decided to do with my new life — and she gave me some invaluable advice about computers and programs. They all spoke excellent English and swapped between English, French and Dutch with an ease that made us feel ashamed of our struggles to master just one new language.

We thought that with a start like this, 1996 had a lot going for it already.

We got up at 10.45am — slowly. We were lethargic but not hung over. Paul returned our dining chairs and Jack collected one of theirs which he had inadvertently broken by leaning too hard against the back. He mended it with plastic wood, glue and brown shoe polish.

We needed to blow the cobwebs away so we decided to put on our wellingtons and explore the little lane to the right of our house. It split into a Y after about 100 yards but one side was always so overgrown and muddy in summer that it was impossible to navigate. The brambles and vegetation had now died back and it was very inviting.

For part of the way the path was also the bed of a stream and although the ground was generally frozen hard, it was pretty muddy. We sank up to our ankles in the ooze and pebbles.

For the first time we were going round the back of our next-door neighbour's land. We could see both our houses and parts of his field we had never seen before. The orchard trees grew in regimented lines in keeping with the impeccable neatness of his home. He lived in the north of France but had inherited the house, which he had modernised tastefully and visited for holidays. We had occasional stilted conversations, but the family usually kept themselves to themselves behind their locked metal gates.

The path meandered between fields which seemed so unfamiliar from this angle that we could have been anywhere — not a quarter of a mile from home. Just before it split into two and petered out, we stumbled across an enamelled memorial reading "Pierre Bouziat 1920-1946". There was no other information and we wondered why it had been erected in such an obscure place. Then we realised, sadly, that in 1946 this had probably been a busy route frequented by local people and their animals, and that rural depopulation had led to its current sorry state.

We came back through our own field and discovered that Georges had surrounded it with an electric fence, presumably to keep the bull and his family out. He had put a new "gate" at the entrance devised from a tall felled sapling tied to the gate-posts. In spite of this there were still a few cowpats in the grass.

In the late afternoon we made a start on the bathroom. It was on our conscience. We should have done it the previous June but we somehow kept putting it off. We scraped out the bad plaster and disturbed a big black spider which disappeared crossly into a crevice and occasionally waved a big black leg out of the gap. He was not pleased to see the interesting holes in his wall being smoothed off with plaster.

Jack took the windows off and repaired the worst damage to the oak frames. Then he put washers on the hinges to raise them and stop the windows catching. While he was doing this I cleared the attic immediately above the ceiling so that he could break through the floorboards and install an electric light. As I moved all the junk to one side I found a box of 90-year-old medicine bottles and yet another jawbone. No-one had yet been able to explain why the former occupiers of the house might have kept these bones. There were also half a dozen mud and wicker cones for catching swarms of bees.

One job I had been looking forward to was varnishing the floor in the yellow bedroom. We had bought the dark walnut stain on a previous visit. The instructions on the large container said the treated surface could be recoated after it dried in 12 hours. I thought I would do half the room that night and the other half in the morning when it was dry. It was so cold that it took three days for the first half to dry and even then it was tacky in places.

We worked away for the next day on boring but worthy things and had big plans for what we could get done on the Wednesday. Jack spent hours wiring up the electrical gubbins we had bought on the Saturday and puzzling over why it did not seem to have connections where he expected them. He had specified exactly what he wanted for a three-phase supply. When he switched it all on nothing happened and eventually he concluded that he had been sold the wrong part. He had to disconnect it and we went back to the shop on Wednesday afternoon. They conceded that it was indeed not what he wanted but said they would have to get a replacement from another branch which was going to be even more expensive. It wasn't worth coming home so we had to kick our heels for hours in the county town. One good thing was that I persuaded Jack to let me buy a new vacuum cleaner from another DIY merchant. They were on special offer and were of the robust wet 'n' dry variety. Our cylinder hoover at the house was about 30 years old and had been "acquired" from the attic of my old newspaper office where it had been abandoned by a previous tenant who had set up a doomed business as an office cleaner. Its vacuum was suspect and it drove me wild with frustration. In fact, it took me half an hour to hoover the carpet tiles in the kitchen. When I got the new one home and assembled it, it did the job in five minutes. It was pure bliss.

Because Jack had been held up with the fusebox wiring, I had felt able to indulge myself with the Claude Michelet books, whose English titles were "Firelight and Woodsmoke", "Applewood" and "Scent of Herbs." I had read the first two at home in Cheshire and had been enchanted by their descriptions of country life in the pre-war Limousin. Particularly fascinating were the accounts of farming methods (we had many of the implements in the attic), the way of life (their farm sounded much like ours), the local campaign to obtain a railway line (ours had been the lifeblood of the region) and the introduction of electricity — whose technological impact had far outweighed the aesthetics of its installation (as we knew from our "Heath Robinson" wiring).

Jack spent much of the following day rewiring the wiring he had done already for the fuse box. It all fitted together logically this time and although he resented the waste of time he was pleased with the finished job. I worked on bits of the bedroom floor and in slack moments unashamedly lost myself in my Claude Michelet book.

Marguerite was very quiet. When I remonstrated with her she replied: "I have given you three books to go at, what more do you want? They describe everything about life here that I could tell you." She was right. The trilogy was absolutely fascinating and made her world come alive. I kept reading parts of the books aloud to Jack, determined that his vision should be as vivid as mine.

I told him how farmers had progressed from oxen to horses as their beasts of labour and finally turned to tractors — which could do the work in a fraction of the time but impacted the soil with their weight and caused problems of their own. How villages such as ours had once had their bistro, priest, inn, bakery, thriving farms and craftsmen, only to wither away as young people turned from the land. How in 1900 wolves were still roaming the forests. How once every inch of farmland had been cultivated and cared for, providing a cash crop of vegetables which were transported to Paris via the railways. Now these areas lay fallow or sustained a few cattle.

We loved St Paradis but grieved for the changes which had dealt it a body-blow. We had come in as foreigners but we were determined to help keep it alive, even if Fate had decided that its future role would be different. Its heyday had lasted for perhaps a hundred years. We would not let the village die. One day, we promised ourselves, we would think of a project to help breathe life back into it — if we could cope with the draconian French laws for setting up a business.

We were deeply in love with the house and still could not believe our good fortune in finding it, or being found by it. At St Paradis we were able to forget our troubles, relax and truly be ourselves. Our friendships were intense because they were cross-cultural and did not rely on language or the usual social weighing-up. They were at a very human level which relied on smiling, touching and mutual practical aid. Village life anywhere can be a morass of petty squabbles and lifelong animosities. We had come along with a clean sheet and had been absorbed by all sides because we had no preconceptions about them. For its inhabitants, St Paradis might not be heavenly. It had the usual French rural problems of unemployment and alcoholism, for a start, but for us it really was a sort of earthly paradise.

I painted the bathroom ceiling. I had been avoiding this because I was afraid that it too was coated with distemper and that I would have to seal it — the most unpleasant job of all, like painting with sticky water running down your arm. Then I discovered that the original decorators had been amazingly lazy and devious. They had painted the bathroom walls pink with distemper but they had left the ceiling as untouched white plaster. It only took a few minutes with a wide brush to transform the 6ft x 9ft area into a brilliant white vision of cleanliness and modernity.

Flushed with success, and at eight o'clock at night, I decided to paint the kitchen. It was a tad bigger. Each wall measured at least 18ft x 8ft. But I was on a roll and determined to set the task in hand.

The Dulux matt white covered like a dream. The kitchen had a strange colour scheme whereby the bottom third of the walls was painted grey, presumably to mask any dirt the farming family might bring into the house on their boots. It was practical but ugly and made the room very dark. The upper two thirds of the walls had once been white but this had weathered to a dirty cream. The texture varied from rough, where the wall covering was ancient lime mixture, to smooth, where damaged lime had been covered by 20th century plaster. It appeared that Marguerite's parents had only been able to afford to have the worst parts repaired and had left the rest in its pitted state. The contrast between the two was accentuated by the shadows in the grubby cream paint.

The modern matt emulsion covered the textural joins and made them less evident. It went straight over the grey with no underlying difference in colour. As I worked my way slowly round the kitchen it was transformed from pre-war squalor to 1990s cleanliness, without losing the character of the room. I stopped painting when I could no longer focus properly at about 1.30am.

I spent the next day painting. We had invited Paul and Elisabeth over at 7.30pm for our usual last evening get-together and I was determined to finish the job before they arrived.

Jack rewired the sockets in the kitchen using square plastic ducting on the walls for the cables. The plaster was far too fragile to attempt to let the ducting into it. He managed to drill a hole through one of the 20-inch granite blocks framing the front door and installed a carriage-lamp outside to illuminate the front of the house. Annoyingly, it would only take a 60-watt bulb, but this was better than nothing. At night the blackness was total. We had a municipal street light on the end of the barn but it was lit so erratically that no-one could count on it. Villagers simply used torches if they needed to move around after dark.

While we were enjoying a pre-lunch *aperitif* with Paul and Elisabeth, our host disappeared and tottered back into the room proudly with a present for us. It was an enormous bright orange pumpkin which he had grown himself and must have weighed several kilos.

We thanked him and I asked Elisabeth how to cook it. She said it could be roast or boiled like potatoes but she admonished Paul for giving us such a big one. How on earth were we going to eat it between only two of us, she asked. He brushed the criticism aside. It was his pride and joy, the best of the carefully-nurtured crop, and he wanted us to have it. It was an honour. We accepted it in that spirit.

I painted all afternoon while Jack did the wiring. The old plaster was so thirsty that it soaked up many litres of paint and required repeated applications over very small areas. It was slow going. I put the last lick of emulsion on the wall by the front door at 7.25pm, dashed upstairs to change from my boiler suit and welcomed Paul and Elisabeth at 7.30pm with respectable clothes, combed hair and a slurp of make-up.

They were suitably bowled over by the transformation of the kitchen. It was so light and clean that it seemed like a different room. Paul was also impressed by Jack's electrical work.

As the conversation meandered along around the topic of kitchens we decided to measure the bread oven and discovered that it was 2.2 metres deep — surely far larger than would have been necessary for one family's needs.

Then Paul told us about an acquaintance in a nearby farmhouse who filled his kitchen with sheep, pigs, fowl and seven cats. We thought it likely that he really needed to have grey paint as the dominant decor!

But the best part of the evening was when Elisabeth told us that everyone in St Paradis got excited when they knew "Les Anglais" were arriving. When we had come to view the house 18 months earlier, Michel and his wife had told the Leprechaun "We do hope they will buy it and repopulate the village." Now it seemed that we had become like a speck of dust in the oyster: we had brought the promise of a small dynasty of Loaders at the formerly deserted principal house in St Paradis and we had given all our new friends a mutual talking point. They felt we had contributed something to the community, but we knew that we would be forever in their debt.

Paul and Elisabeth could not have given us a better Christmas present. It was a heart-warming way to welcome in the New Year together.

At 11 o'clock the next morning I was in our bedroom packing the suitcases when some movement in the road caught my eye. I glanced round and saw what I thought was a very large light-brown dog wandering along the grass verge. I took a closer look and discovered that it was a calf. It was accompanied by its twin brother, its big sister, its mother — and its father.

I raced downstairs to Jack and we stood outside the front door watching as the bull led his little family over the wall by the well and into the field. The makeshift gate and the electric fence had proved to be no deterrent at all.

It was not the same bull as before. The first patriarch had been massive and battle-scarred, with a harem of wives. This was a young animal, still putting on weight and gravitas, and currently monogamous.

The little group settled down happily and we did not disturb them.

We liked having a bull by the back door.

What does the French mean?

Acte de vente (nf)	final house sale contract
Anciens francs (nm)	old francs (100 x new francs)
Auberge (nf)	inn
Bon viveur (nm)	jovial; enjoys life
Boudoir (nm)	lady's bedroom
Boulangerie (nf)	baker's shop
Bricolage (nm)	DIY superstore
Cantou (nm)	special large Limousin fireplace
Chambres d'hôte (nf)	bed and breakfast
Compromis de vente (nm)	first house sale contract (promise to buy)
Disparu (adj)	missing
Echelle (nf)	ladder
Fenêtre (nf)	window
Fermette (nf)	farmhouse-style cottage
La France Profonde (nf)	Deepest (rural) France
Gîte (nm)	rented holiday home
Ma petite (nf)	my little one
Maire (nm)	mayor
Mairie (nf)	town hall
Maquis (nm)	bands of Resistance fighters
Merci (excl)	thank you
Mort en déportation (adj)	died in concentration camp
Notaire (nm)	government lawyer
Oh la la! (excl)	all-purpose exclamation
Papier maché (nm)	made of pulped paper

Passe-partout (nm)	picture framing method popular in 1920s
Porte (nf)	door
Regrets	on tombstone – greatly missed
Rentrée (nf)	"Back to School"; Autumn season
Reservé (adj)	reserved (for someone)
Résistant (nm)	member of Resistance
Rideau (nm)	curtain
S'il vous plait	please
Sabot (nm)	wooden clog
Tapis (nm)	carpet
Taxe fonçiere (nf)	local property tax
Taxe d'habitation (nf)	local council tax
Toute suite	straight away
Vous n'êtes pas étrangers	You're not strangers/outsiders

ONLY FOOLS DRINK WATER
Written by GEOFFFREY MORRIS and illustrated by PATRICIA KELSALL

"...We sat down for lunch after a hot and strenuous morning gathering in the straw. I was distressingly dehydrated. Pitchers of water stood ready to dilute the *pastis* to individual taste. The temptation was too great for me. I reached for a water jug and filled an empty glass to the brim. It had barely touched my parched lips when cries of consternation and incredulity came from all sides.

"That's water! WATER, I tell you!"

"You'll derange yourself!"

"Don't you know the harm straight water can do?"

"You can't drink it like that!"

"You've put it in the wrong glass. There's your *pastis*!"

There was even a serious appeal from one of the helpers who thought that I spoke no French.

"Do something! Stop him! He'll do himself a mischief! These *sacré* foreigners have no idea how to look after their health!"

It was as though I had brought out a hip flask of whisky at a total abstainers' convention..."

The author and his wife – jokingly dubbed "senile delinquents" by their long-suffering son – have been enjoying hilarious escapades in the Charente-Maritime marshlands of France for more than 40 years. They have lived there for 20 years and are now naturalised French. This delightful book describes their experiences.

Price £8.99   ISBN 1 901253 10 4

AN IMPRINT OF
ANNE LOADER
PUBLICATIONS

**From Anne Loader Publications, 13 Vale Road,
Hartford, Northwich, Cheshire CW8 1PL
Please add £1.30 to cover carriage
E-mail: anne@leoniepress.com
Website: www.leoniepress.com**

**An imprint of
ANNE LOADER
PUBLICATIONS**

Other books published by the Léonie Press, an imprint of Anne Loader Publications, 13 Vale Road, Hartford, Northwich, Cheshire CW8 1PL, Gt Britain, include:

Memories of a Cheshire Childhood by Lenna Bickerton (Memorial edition ISBN 1 901253 13 9), price £4.99

A House with Sprit: A dedication to Marbury Hall by Jackie Hamlett and Christine Hamlett (ISBN 1 901253 19 8), price £8.99

Kathleen: Memories of a girl who grew up in wartime by K M Thomas (ISBN 1 901253 02 3), price £5.99

Ulu Tiram: A cameo of life in Malaya at the time of 'The Emergency' by Peter Thomas and Kathleen Thomas (ISBN 1 901253 05 8), price £5.75

A Nun's Grave: A Novel set in the Vale Royal of England by Alan K Leicester (ISBN 1 901253 08 5), price £7.99

The Way We Were: Omnibus edition of Les Cooper's Crewe memories 'Over My Shoulder' and 'Another's War' by Les Cooper (ISBN 1 901253 07 4), price £7.99

The Duck with a Dirty Laugh: More family adventures in rural France by Anne Loader (ISBN 1 901253 35 X), price £8.99

For the full list, visit our website: www.leoniepress.com